PRAISE FOR *I D* *WHO I AM ANYMORE*

"This book is a gift to anyone who feels like they've lost themselves after heartbreak and loss changes everything they see. *I Don't Know Who I Am Anymore* is a warm hug you don't want to miss!"

—AMANDA BACON, PROVERBS 31 MINISTRIES, COAUTHOR
OF *SHINY THINGS*, COHOST OF THE *ALL THE MOM THINGS*
PODCAST, AND HOST OF THE *AT NIGHT* PODCAST

"I loved this book. Carole Holiday's wonderful personality, wit, and wisdom come through on every page. Plus, there is help on every page for all of us who have experienced grief."

—JIM BURNS, PHD, PRESIDENT OF HOMEWORD AND
AUTHOR OF *DOING LIFE WITH YOUR ADULT CHILDREN*

"Carole Holiday's that person who finishes your sentences, gives you the safe space you need to cry, and somehow makes you giggle out loud even when you're hurting. You're in for an adventure of healing through savoring these pages. In the presence of someone like Carole, who listens and understands, you'll *find who you are again.*"

—DR. SHERI KEFFER, RELATIONSHIP THERAPIST
AND AUTHOR OF *INTIMATE DECEPTION*

"I was unable to put this book down. Carole's writing is stunning and superb. A must-read for anyone struggling in their faith, struggling with identity after loss, or really anyone who seeks to better answer the question 'why do bad things happen to good people?'"

—LAURA LAWSON VISCONTI, COFOUNDER DRINK COFFEE
DO STUFF AND AUTHOR OF *BELIEVING IS SEEING*

"In this thoughtful book, Carole helps us find our way Home by giving language to the voices that dwell in the deepest chambers of our wounded souls—a place where only God can commune with us through our suffering and in our pain."

—Virginia Dixon, founder and CEO of Tender Hearts
Enterprises, author, leader, and speaker

"Whimsically written but poignantly true reflections on grief and loss, this book isn't a field guide to finding yourself but a map back to the very heart of God. Encapsulating the essence of the gospel—dead things being made alive—Carole's words are a healing salve of truth and encouragement."

—Meredith Boggs, author of The Journey Home

"Carole Holiday understands how grief, heartache, and pain can make us feel invisible, unloved, or unworthy. But she also understands how God can heal our hearts and help us find our way back to who we are according to Him. With vulnerable wit and wisdom (and some really good recipes!) Carole takes your hand and walks with you toward the One who can give you hope."

—Donna Jones, author and pastor's wife

"As a pastor, I am aware that some of the most comforting words I can give (and receive) are 'I'm with you' and 'I understand.' Carole Holiday whispers this page after page in vivid, honest pictures of real life and divine hope and encouragement. Let her walk with you. Let her make food for you. And take courage—'there is healing ahead.'"

—Chad Halliburton, lead pastor of Oakhouse Church

"Even if you're not in the midst of a trial, you will count this as a good read and a book worth sharing with friends who are. Well done for a first-time author. Wounded but recovering."

—Michael Mizrahi, award winning
author of The Unnamed Girl

"If you or someone you know is ensnared in the grip of grief, Carole meets you where you are and walks alongside you on your path toward healing. Together, you'll cry, laugh, and deepen your faith as you pursue wholeness and healing after loss, and enjoy some wonderful comfort food along the way!"

—Traci Morrow, author of Real-Life Marriage, wellness coach, and relationship guide for Maxwell Leadership

"Within the depths of grief and loss our identities can become unrecognizable, leaving us feeling adrift and disconnected from ourselves. By weaving together her personal story, biblical insights, practical learnings, and soul-nourishing recipes, Carole offers the reader solace, understanding, and hope that comforts like a warm embrace, reassuring us that we are not alone in our suffering."

—Danielle Kemp, senior pastor of Reconcile Church

"Read this book . . . metabolize its contents (Thanks, Eugene Peterson!) . . . then SHARE this book. Grief is a journey . . . invite Carole Holiday to join you in your journey."

—Tim Robertson, associate pastor of New Life Church

"This book is the giant hug we all need while going through life's toughest seasons. Carole's approach is comprehensive and empathetic, and I love how she integrates scripture into the healing journey. I would highly recommend this book to anyone who is experiencing grief or supporting someone who is."

—Rachael H. Elmore, MA, LCMHC-S, NCC, author of A Mom Is Born and licensed mental health counselor

"Reading this book is like cherished one-on-one time with my friend. It's a conversation—give and take. It is a gift. As is Carole Holiday."

—Ken Kemp, author of Why Not Today, podcaster, and pastor

"I was hooked on the first page. This girl is real. Loss, discovering betrayal, going through it with her kids, grandkids, and coming out shining through her growing faith in Jesus Christ. Do yourself a life-changing favor and READ this book. I read it straight through."

I DON'T KNOW WHO
I AM ANYMORE

RESTORING YOUR IDENTITY
SHATTERED BY GRIEF AND LOSS

CAROLE HOLIDAY

NELSON
BOOKS

An Imprint of Thomas Nelson

Published in Nashville, Tennessee, by Nelson Books, an imprint of Thomas Nelson. Nelson Books and Thomas Nelson are registered trademarks of HarperCollins Christian Publishing, Inc.

Published in association with COMPEL, a writers community founded by Lysa TerKeurst.

Published in association with the literary agency of Brock, Inc., P.O. Box 384, Matthews, NC 28105.

Thomas Nelson titles may be purchased in bulk for educational, business, fundraising, or sales promotional use. For information, please email SpecialMarkets@ThomasNelson.com.

Library of Congress Cataloging-in-Publication Data

Names: Holiday, Carole, author.
Title: I don't know who I am anymore : restoring your identity shattered by grief and loss / Carole Holiday.
Description: Nashville, Tennessee : Nelson Books, [2023] | Summary: "No stranger to heartache, Carole Holiday artfully braids together her story of overwhelming loss with biblical insights and delicious recipes from the little cottage on the lane--the cooking school she once owned. Carole's journey offers hope that after the ravages of grief and despair, God can bring good back to life through faith, food, and fellowship"--Provided by publisher.
Identifiers: LCCN 2023010749 (print) | LCCN 2023010750 (ebook) | ISBN 9781400239399 (paperback) | ISBN 9781400239405 (ebook)
Subjects: LCSH: Grief--Religious aspects--Christianity. | Holiday, Carole--Religion. | Businesspeople--United States --Religious life. | Cooking. | LCGFT: Cookbooks.
Classification: LCC BV4905.3 .H65 2023 (print) | LCC BV4905.3 (ebook) | DDC 248.8/6--dc23/eng/20230525
LC record available at https://lccn.loc.gov/2023010749
LC ebook record available at https://lccn.loc.gov/2023010750

Printed in the United States of America

23 24 25 26 27 LBC 5 4 3 2 1

To my three children, Taylor, Kendall, and KC.

When I saw only darkness, you brought the light. When I felt like life wasn't worth living, I saw your faces. When I didn't know who I was anymore, you reminded me.

This is gold—the ore of relationships mined in trials and tribulations that test us and strangely bring out the best in us too. It's one of life's great mysteries, as is your love for me.

And to Amanda-Leigh, Tommy, and Bryony Grace, you make those three humans even better. I love you like you were my own, and I love your littles so much that my heart hurts (in a good way).

CONTENTS

CONTENTS

FIRST THOUGHTS

THIS IS A STORY ABOUT GRIEF AND THE JOURNEY OUT OF IT.

There was a season in my life when losses came so fast and furiously that I found myself saying out loud, "I don't know who I am anymore." Grief had swept away my sense of self and left me feeling raw and worthless.

Thankfully, that's not the end of the story but the beginning of a new one.

There is no quick fix for relieving the pain of grief and no timeline to tell you how long it will take. But I share the things that helped me in hopes that they can help you too.

Part story. Part Scripture. Part solution.

I use the words of Jesus, well, simply because I believe them to be life-giving and real. If you don't think of Him as holy, then think of His words as ones of wisdom and encouragement. All the greatest spiritual leaders in the world's religions have repeated and revered them.

Most importantly, this story is not just about me, but it's about you, dear reader. If you are grieving—reeling from life's losses, disappointments, or heartaches—I hope that this encourages. If you have a loved one who is grieving, I pray that the loss can be softened.

In my darkest days, I never thought the nightmare would end. I can tell you that it has, and I desperately want you to experience the same freedom.

———————

When, Lord, when? When will You redeem?
　　When will You see me? When will You hear me?
I write for all of us.

The wanderers, the woebegone, the wayward, the widows and widowers, those wavering in faith, the waylaid. The wonderless. The weak. The worthless. Those who weep and wail. Those who have lost their will.

　　Those without.

This book is for you and about you. There is healing ahead.

INTRODUCTION

TOO MANY TO COUNT

*She touched the grime of her tear-soaked hair. The mud clung
to the strands twisting its beauty into the dirt from the road.
It decorated her face in wandering paths where the tears tore
through her veil of mud, cleansing the unclean. With the holy
breath inside of her restored; the Imago Dei could now be seen.*
—BONNIE LEWIS

HELLO, TEARS. DON'T YOU HAVE SOMEPLACE ELSE TO GO?

Actually, no. They don't. They stay. Stubbornly. Persistently. Endlessly. Setting up permanent residence in the house of our angst, proudly bearing the visible sign of our invisible grief. Like a giant billboard plastered high on the corner of Hollywood and Vine. You've heard of that street corner, right? The one not far from Schwab's Soda Fountain, where stars were born when luck collided with good looks and a talent scout from nearby Paramount Pictures. (Before reality TV made *real* celebrities like we have today.)

I remember crying so much, for so long, that one side of my brain started talking to the other, debating with deep discontent and dismay over why I had not learned such things in my college anatomy course. Where is this saltwater reservoir of such endless supply? Surely it must be hidden in the vicinity of the heart, masquerading as a pancreas or liver or diaphragm. What is a diaphragm even good for anyway if you are not an opera singer or in Miss Rose Richards's Glee Club class, where she admonished us, in vain, to "Breathe from your diaphragm, ladies"?

Then there's the weirdness of forever wondering, *How can the body keep making these tears?* The irony bewitched me. I mean, this water flowed so freely from a place of dire desolation and bone-dry drought. Like a divining rod had dipped downward between the cactus and the tumbleweed blowing across my soul, marking an underground artesian well. I imagined a perpetual stream of water springing from its source, cutting a crooked path through the naked hillside with a steady rivulet.

Rivulet . . . don't you love that word? I think the ancient king David understood about rivulets and cutting and crooked paths on naked hillsides. I think David knew how that felt.

These are his words:

> I am worn out from my groaning.
>
> All night long I flood my bed with weeping
> and drench my couch with tears.
>
> (PSALM 6:6)

David knew that sometimes the tears just wouldn't stop.

Hello, tears. Don't you have someplace else to go?

Undoubtedly, the dinner guests whispered that among themselves (and in the direction of the shadowy figure). It was outdoor dining at its pre-COVID best, with candlelight and night-blooming jasmine trailing overhead. In his gospel account, Luke inferred that the best

wine was uncorked, the VIPs were dressed to the nines in their orna-
mental robes, and the evening's entertainment was set to begin. That
"strange one," Jesus, had reclined at the low table comfortably, which
signaled to the host that they were off to an auspicious start. He was
settling in to stay a spell.

But then she slid into the room. From the edges of the town to
the edges of the table, she skulked. The dregs of society sometimes
pooled on the perimeter of the wealthy's feasts, eavesdropping on the
elite conversations and hoping for scraps at the end of the party, but
this was a new form of boldness. Audacious. Scandalous. Awkward.
Just like tears can be. So darn awkward.

Shaking, she searched for Jesus in the crowded space. Skirting
the disapproving stares and muttered slurs, she fell to the floor beside
Him and washed His feet with her tears. You might ask, *How many
tears does it take to wash feet?* Too many to count. A rivulet cutting a
crooked path through His naked feet, a perpetual stream of water
springing from its source.

The texts describe the woman as a prostitute, by all accounts
a victim of her own sinful choices, deserving the ostracism she
endured. An invisible woman—a persona non grata of the human
race, erased by her own wayward ways. No one else to blame. As
we read the story, we tolerate her interruption just slightly more
than did the Pharisees seated at the table. We cringe when we get
to the part about the woman letting down her locks and her hair
wiping at the dirt caked on Jesus' feet. This is awkward. Really
awkward. How do we explain *this* to the junior high Sunday school
class?

The cultural narrative hints at more, though, and author Bonnie
Lewis gives us insight through a different lens. What if we renamed
this woman with contemporary language such as "sex trafficked"?[1]
Would it color our understanding of her story? By Lewis's interpretation, the woman is seeking love and escape and freedom, but

she has been so emotionally, sexually, and verbally abused that the only way she knows how to communicate is through this socially provocative body language that has, up until now, ensured her survival. As sorrowful as it is, her worth has been distilled down to one thing.

And it's her hair—the symbol of that one thing—that she is wetting with her endless tears to wipe her slate clean. Hot tears cleansing hot sins.

An invisible woman. But maybe, just maybe, she could offer Him this. Then maybe He would see her. When the tears freely flow, desperation leaves us searching for something we have of value to barter or trade for our peace and happiness.

Jesus' response?

"Whoever has been forgiven little loves little" (Luke 7:47). That's for you, Mr. Pharisee. This is the part of the story when the high-on-his-high-horse host shrinks back into his tunic and hangs his head in his hummus.

And to the woman coiled at His feet, Jesus lifted her head simultaneously with her stature, upending the power structures at hand and bestowing upon her favor in the eyes of her oppressors. Jesus assured her that her many sins, now forgiven, had made room for her to love deeply and with abandon (vv. 36–50).

I like to think that this is also true of grief, and it applies to our losses too. Those who have grieved deeply possess an enormous capacity to love deeply, exactly because of the enormous space that the grief

> Those who have grieved deeply possess an enormous capacity to love deeply, exactly because of the enormous space that the grief rented and will someday vacate.

rented and will someday vacate. This should instill immense hope in the hearts of those who hurt.

When sorrow is close, and we read Luke's words describing the woman's desperation, we're instantly transported back to our own moments of desperation. When breathing seemed secondary to the anguish of our hearts and gasping for air mixed with cries from some deep place we didn't know existed. It seemed as if everything inside melted, and our very souls were seeping out the underside of our shoes.

I remember those moments of desperation, as I'm sure you remember yours.

Raw moments, which for me at once confounded and confused. Moments strangely blurred by the fast-forward motion that hurtled me into the unknown, yet simultaneously stopping time as if I had been caught in the glistening web of an expectant spider.

Moments when I became that invisible woman, not knowing who I was.

With the discovery of an intimate betrayal, I simply disappeared. The secret emails that I stumbled upon only confirmed that notion of me, as their content suggested that I didn't exist at all. Surely these words could not be his. And could those possibly be *hers*? The one who had caused such extraordinary, indescribable pain in an earlier clandestine relationship ten years ago?

Time and again, I became that invisible woman, not knowing who I was anymore.

It happened in a few raw moments.

Like when the surgeon stood before me when he should've been standing knee-deep in the complex surgery that was going to save my best friend—the friend who was the safe and solid Rock of Gibraltar for our family. When the doctor shook his head and uttered the words, "I'm so sorry," I gave in to the sadness that weighed me down. All eyes in the huge university hospital waiting area followed me, drenched as I was with despair. I reminded them of the outcome they hoped never to hear. In my peripheral vision, I spied the emotional support dog and his handler making a beeline to my corner like a bird dog coming for its lifeless prey.

I was that invisible woman.

In a few more raw moments, getting the "thanks, but goodbye" from a job I had done well. Erased from a position that I performed with pride. Feeling unable to make up the gap in the one-income household I now maintained.

I was that invisible woman.

In a few remaining raw moments, when I sat in the courtroom to declare my financial insolvency. *Bankruptcy.* Even now, I choke on that word. I spied someone I knew and I prayed to fade into the woodwork and shrivel with shame. I couldn't help but wonder what my late father would think. My father, who oversaw the budget for the city of Los Angeles for many years and never paid a bill late in his life. I wanted to hide from him, if only in my memories.

I was that invisible woman when my doctor explained more extensive tests were necessary, and I wagered that my prayers to die might be rewarded after all. By this time I was wanting to be invisible and wondered if this was my way out of my pain.

Time and again, I was that invisible woman, that persona non grata. Now, coiled at the feet of Jesus, I hoped the tears might cleanse, might heal, might free me from the grief. The newly discovered affair, job loss, bankruptcy, heart failure, inoperable cancer, all a molten river liquidating my insides and finishing me off with a white-hot hollowing-out.

Raw moments erase innocence, covenants and precious promises, health, emotional stability, relationships, financial soundness. It felt like a rising tide, hungry to carry me along with it.

And all the while, the tears wouldn't stop. They just wouldn't stop.

Hello, tears. Please tell me you have someplace else to go.

My chest squeezes tightly as I type this, praying for the person who is reading these words and realizing, *I guess I'm not the only one.* Pain partners strangers who stumble together along a path of healing that was never part of anyone's plan. Wait! Who decided this detour in our perfectly plotted itinerary?

> Pain partners strangers who stumble along a path of healing together that was never part of anyone's plan.

For the tears that won't stop and the pain that is palpable, God redeems. He meets us at the end of ourselves with promises of renewal and restoration when our identity and worth have been swept away by an avalanche of loss. For whomever whispers, "That's me," there is hope on the other side of grief.

As an adult, the first time I remembered not being able to stop the tears was when I was a senior in college. That was the year I spied the request in the printed church bulletin. (Remember those?) I don't recall the exact wording, but a family was asking for help with meals because their young son, Derek, had cancer. Needless to say, meal planning falls down the priority list in a household suffering in this way. As a new wife who liked to cook, I imagined it would be an easy role to fill. I thought back to my childhood, the time my mom sent me across the street to a grieving neighbor with a foil-covered roast beef and a note in her familiar cursive hand: "For the boys' lunches." When you grieve, you cook. When others grieve, you cook for them.

Derek was the cutest kid I had ever seen—adorable and brimming with life when we first met. When I asked his mom what he liked to eat, she laughed and answered, "Beef burgundy." But she crumpled her nose and in her melodic Southern accent drawled, "It's so funny the way that Derek says it though. 'Bo-eff bur-gone-*YON*.' Every syllable emphasized as a proper Frenchman would."

Well, I learned to make "bo-eff bur-gone-*YON*" and delivered it to Derek, along with incessant tears and passionate prayers for healing. Our healing prayers for Derek never materialized, as hard as we prayed. And, to this day, I think of him whenever I see beef burgundy on a menu or plan it as an entrée for an autumn dinner party. Derek is always in the background, laughing and running through the house, skillfully enunciating, "bo-eff bur-gone-*YON*." I have learned to smile at the memory of that energetic little boy, but shadows hover and I say a prayer for that lovely mommy with the melodic Southern accent.

What happens when the prayers we so fervently pray go unanswered? What happens when the finances fail, when the husband doesn't come back, when the reputation is slandered and lies replace truth? What happens when you bury your beloved little boy?

What do we, as followers of Jesus, do when we don't get our happily-ever-after ending?

Derek changed that for me. After him, I saw a need to welcome a real space for lament into the heart of worship. Perhaps that absence of lament is why no one ever stood up in church and said, "I'm praising God tonight, *even though* _____." Fill in the blank. I wondered if I—if we—were capable of that. Would I have a test of that someday in my own life?

Perhaps it was at that moment that God started to lay groundwork for my future. Perhaps He wanted me to wrestle with this notion that a loving, magnanimous, generous Father would allow pain in my life. Perhaps loss wasn't for some ancient story about a beautifully tressed but broken soul named Mary or a deeply sorrowful king named David. Perhaps He was "preheating my heart" to accept what was going into the oven for me.

We'll consider those questions together in the pages ahead. This book will hold an honest account of angst, perhaps similar to yours, perhaps not. But loss takes on a strange similarity when it comes to its consequences. The wake your sorrows leave looks very much like mine. Best of all, though, we'll review promises and practices to reset our foundation in *imago Dei*—the image of God—taking us on a journey from "invisible" women to women over whom the Creator of the universe rejoices.

———————

On some of my darkest days, which looked a bit more like dusk than dawn for my kids, too, I would text my youngest son these words: "Something good's gonna happen for you tomorrow, KC Holiday." It was my love letter to him, wanting him to believe, even if I didn't, that something good was gonna happen. And, in the beginning, I rarely believed.

I'd like you to imagine that I am texting you that same message. That wherever you are right now, whether you believe it or not, that something good is about to happen in your life.

It's God's mystery that He promises more for us. We see veiled now, but nothing can prepare us for what He has for us.

As it is written:
"What no eye has seen,
what no ear has heard,
and what no human mind has conceived"—
the things God has prepared for those who love him.

(1 CORINTHIANS 2:9)

My Sunday school teacher said so. Mrs. Winchell. The one with the brain tumor.

But that's a story for another day.

LAUGHTER AND LEMONADE

For ten years I owned a cooking school in a historic district of Southern California. I am not a professional cook, and our motto reflected that: "We're not chefs, and neither are you." Somehow, though, in a rose-covered cottage at the end of a lazy lane, hundreds of guests savored hundreds of meals served on my grandmother's Limoges china. The garden overflowed with laughter and lemonade, along with fresh herbs and sweet peas, a favorite flower of my grandfather, who taught me some of my favorite recipes. I loved cooking, but more than that, I loved the experience of sharing meals and conversation around a common table.

Often, friends brought friends who were in deep grief, sometimes on their first outing after a loss, and I simultaneously taught and prayed for the brokenhearted one as we served the soup. I always believed there was healing around the table. I still do. Our thought was, *Feed the soul first. The stomach will happily follow.*

When writing this book, I didn't expect to include recipes. *That was not a plan of mine.* (By the way, this will not be the first time you see that phrase.) But, as I recalled specific stories about grief, certain dishes popped into my head, and it felt natural to include them. That just sort of happened—much like my story, and like so many seren-dipities along the way of its telling. I hope you enjoy these.

Derek's Boeuf Bourguignon

Also known as Beef Burgundy

I always envision sharing this meal fireside with a crusty French loaf and a little bit of merlot. It's the perfect dish for deep conversation and long lingering.

A provincial dish from the Burgundy region—meaning rustic, country—like what Belle from *Beauty and the Beast* would have made for Gaston if he hadn't been such a raving narcissist.

This dish is not hard, but it is slow. Don't be put off by the steps—just make it on a day that you plan to spend at home. And it's better two to three days later after the flavors in the dish deepen, so it's a perfect do-ahead company meal. Much like grief's resolution, good things take time.

BOUQUET GARNI (OR LITTLE BAG OF HERBS AND VEGGIES)

- 1 carrot, roughly chopped
- 1 medium onion, peeled and quartered
- 3 cloves garlic, smashed
- 1 sprig fresh thyme
- 3 bay leaves
- Stems from the button mushrooms used in the stew

STEW

- 6 slices bacon (a thicker cut is always nice)
- 2 pounds stewing beef
- 1 teaspoon salt

DEREK'S BOEUF BOURGUIGNON

½ teaspoon ground black pepper

1 tablespoon vegetable oil, if needed

1 (750 ml) bottle pinot noir (the red wine traditionally used in this dish)

3 cups beef broth

2 tablespoons tomato paste

6 carrots, cut into 2-inch pieces, preferably cut on the diagonal

½ pound small button mushrooms, stemmed, with stems reserved (halve the mushrooms if large)

1 (14- to 16-ounce) bag frozen white pearl onions* (alternatively, use fresh onions)

2 tablespoons red or black currant jelly

2 tablespoons softened butter mashed with 3 tablespoons all-purpose flour or 1 tablespoon cornstarch mixed with 2 tablespoons water (gluten-free option)

Fresh parsley (optional)

DIRECTIONS

1. Gather all the bouquet garni ingredients together into a piece of cheesecloth and tie with kitchen string.
2. Preheat the oven to 325 degrees.
3. Place the bacon in a deep, heavy-bottomed, oven-proof pot (I use a Staub enameled cast-iron pot) over medium heat and cook until crisp. Remove and set aside for breakfast. Reserve the fat in the pan.
4. Spread out the beef cubes on a paper towel–lined baking sheet and pat dry with a paper towel. (Dry meat browns well.)
5. Sprinkle the beef cubes with the salt and pepper, place them in the pot with the hot bacon grease, and cook until brown on all sides. Work in small batches, using tongs to turn the meat, since crowding the pan will braise the beef, not brown it. If you need to add more fat, add 1 tablespoon of vegetable oil. Transfer the beef cubes to a plate

as they are browned. Any juices that collect will be added back to the pot, so don't use a paper towel to line the plate.

6. Add the browned beef back to the pot along with the meat juices, wine, broth, tomato paste, and carrots. Bring to a boil, scraping the bottom of the pan to lift the flavorful residue stuck on the bottom. Once the stew reaches a boil, turn off the heat and add the bouquet garni. Cover the pot and transfer to the oven. Cook for 2 hours. The alcohol will burn off but deepen the flavors. Your house will smell amazing too!

7. After 2 hours, remove the pot from the oven and carefully transfer the bouquet garni to a bowl. When it is cool enough to handle, squeeze the flavorful juices into the bowl, then pour them back into the pot. (I usually press the bouquet garni with the back of a ladle initially, but when it's cool enough to handle, I squeeze the cheesecloth with my hands to extract as much liquid as possible.)

8. Add the mushrooms, pearl onions, and currant jelly and gently stir to combine. Add the butter-flour or cornstarch-water mixture and stir.

9. Return the pot to the oven for another 30 minutes. You can keep the pot in the oven on a lower heat to keep it warm until dinner. If you wish to thicken the sauce more, simmer it on the stovetop uncovered to reduce the liquid.

10. Serve over mashed potatoes and garnish with chopped parsley if desired.

11. If you decide to make the dish ahead of time, just reheat it an hour before guests arrive.

Makes 6 servings.

Cook's note: To easily peel fresh pearl onions, make a small x at the stem end with a sharp paring knife and place in boiling water for 2 minutes. Remove to a plate to cool. When cool enough to handle, push the onion out of the skin, and slice off the other stem end.

CHAPTER 1

THE NIGHTMARE LIVING IN THE CLOSET

Probably one or two moments in your whole life you will hear
a dark whispering spirit, a voice coming from the center of
things. It will have blades for lips and will not stop until it
speaks the one secret thing at the heart of it all. Kneeling
on the floor, unable to stop shuddering, I heard it plainly.
It said, You are unlovable Lily Owens. Unlovable. Who
could love you? Who in this world could ever love you?

—SUE MONK KIDD

IT RETURNED EVERY NIGHT LIKE CLOCKWORK, STALKING MY SLEEP.
Within its angry visits, a phantom voice sobbed, "I can't find me
anywhere," and not recognizing that as my own cry, I remember
thinking, *That poor, poor girl. She can't find herself anywhere.*

It's one thing not to be able to find your keys, or to be lost without your phone's GPS, or even lost in a sea of confusion, like when
you're trying to buy some simple bottles for your sister's baby shower
and are overwhelmed by the soaring wall of new and improved nipples. But to be lost because you feel as if you've disappeared? To be

lost because no one can see you? To be lost because no one can feel your pain? The stab to my stomach reminds me of how deep a grief that is.

This is not just, "Gee, I don't feel so good about myself today." It's waking up at three o'clock in the morning and googling, "Can human DNA be rearranged?" It's wondering about loss at the cellular level, as if your very own double helixes—those twisted-ladder genetic strands carrying your identity—suddenly unfurl, flapping in the wind. Your DNA, the code that makes you *you*, is picked clean, much like you might hold a sprig of garden rosemary and slide your thumb and forefinger down the stem to strip off the leaves. Denuded. Empty. Used. Discarded. Thrashed and trashed.

Grief is notorious for sweeping in under surprise attack—a party crasher bearing gifts we didn't ask for, which can't be exchanged or returned. Our sense of who we are in the world vanishes, stolen by a thief in the night, along with familiar pillars crumbling under the weight of the uninvited event. Unplanned. Unpromised. Unscheduled. It waylays us. And when the smoke clears, the battleground is littered with casualties from the war between life as you want it to be and life as it is now.

> Grief is notorious for sweeping in under surprise attack.

On one side, in the land of "life as you want it to be," predictability reigns. White picket fences encircle modern farmhouses (preferably flipped by Chip and Jo), showcasing sleek counters, cool art, a good-looking and pedigreed partner, and a Peloton perched in the corner. Add to it the ever-so-humble, teensy-weensy expectation of health and wealth, hand-painted on a weathered barnwood sign centered over the fireplace, two and a half children who adore school and us (not in that order, naturally), a fluffy Fido for the Christmas card (shelter rescue, of course), a trending TikTok account and just enough views to show we count, but not so many as to cast doubt on our humility. Tack on a fat 401(k) and a remote-from-home career shared with a spouse who crafts steamy love letters and perfect matcha lattes every morning after a five-mile jog. Heaven on earth.

On the other side of the tracks, though, where the dry brush grows a bit thicker, in the camp of "life as it is now," just one word ignites our grief. Voilà! Pick one, any one. The weeds draw the spark, and a wildfire erupts, sweeping through the landscape of our lives.

Affair . . . Infidelity . . . Betrayal
ER
Inoperable
Incurable
Cancer
COVID
Bankrupt
Slandered
Subpoenaed
Pink-slipped (or whatever color slip you get when you're fired)
Divorce

Stringing triggering words together, like spiked baubles on a cord, they can cut instantaneously.

"It's over."
"There's someone else."
"I'm sorry. There's nothing we can do."
"We found something on the X-ray that we didn't expect."
"You're ordered to appear."
"We won't be needing you anymore."
"Is there someone you want us to call?"
"He's not coming back."

In the land of moviemaking, that's called an *inciting incident*. It's when the shoe drops, the accident happens, the secret's discovered, or the monster reveals his ugly head, and it's classic screenwriting. Not to ruin Friday's date night, but observe this the next time you watch a movie. Fifteen minutes, or approximately fifteen pages into the script, "something" happens that lights the fuse to the story. Wait for that "something" before you run for the popcorn, because it sets the trajectory of the film. All words written in the script from that point forward propel that primary incident ahead, through arc and character development, conflict, high highs, deep lows, and eventual resolution.

And, by the way, in case you hadn't noticed, resolution doesn't have to mean "happily ever after." That used to be fairly predictable, at least in the Busby Berkeley films of the 1930s where ladies in weird-looking shorts and feathered headdresses danced and sang in fountains and bubbles. Not so much in modern cinema. Now we've grown accustomed to walking out of the theater feeling unsettled or perhaps unhappy and being provoked by the movie's ending. Obviously, film started to mirror real life somewhere along the way. Anyone else relate to unsettled, unhappy, and provoked by our "endings"?

I, for one, will go on record as saying that I like happy endings and would even wear those weird shorts if I thought that guaranteed one for me.

If your story became a screenplay, and you named your inciting incident, what would it be? I'm guessing you can recall its setting in high-resolution 3D. What the room looked like, if it was too cold or too hot, or if the sunshine was casting a warm box of light for the cat on the carpet. You remember the smells lingering from breakfast and the nausea that swept over you. You saw your trembling hands and your ring and the color of the nail polish that had chipped, predictably, off the tip of your left index finger.

4

Every sense stood at attention and hypervigilance took the wheel, despite how you tried, in vain, to get Jesus to take it. Every fiber, every follicle, every nerve ending responded to the "ten-hut!" your brain silently shouted. It was torture. And you could write it down word for word, minute by minute.

If my life were a movie, its inciting incident would read like this.

Two voices. Indistinct arguing. Door slams. Car screeches away.
Wife collapses. Wife's world implodes. Loyal dog licks her face.
END SCENE.

The day after that door slammed, I was "let go" from my job. And in a series of cascading dominoes related to money, health, literal heartbreak and heart surgery, betrayal, divorce, and death, the long line of tin soldiers toppled, and my world marched off with them. I even lost that loyal doggie who licked my face.

Yeah. I'm with Busby. I really do prefer the happy endings.

My phone chimed, signaling a text.

I hear ur writing a book. Is it about your marriage?

My middle child was inquiring.

Scrolling through icons, I selected and then scrubbed the smiley face and opted to answer lickety-split with an all-inclusive thumbs-up emoji. But with a caveat.

Dear Daughter of Divorce, a playfully irreverent reference to "Daughter of Eve," and a nod to our favorite childhood series, the Chronicles of Narnia.

Tap. Tap. Tap. YES.

The answer is yes.

I'm sure she wondered what tales might be told.

This book reveals the death of my marriage, yes, but only because it acts as the simmering soup pot from which my story springs. (Sorry—I think I must've been making a big pot of turkey chili that day.) That sad ending really marks the beginning of a journey to understanding the place, person, and position from which I derived my identity and that had—*snap!*—evaporated in a millisecond.

Last, I typed out: I need this to make sense.

Then I added a smiley face.

True, I did not ask for what happened. You probably didn't ask for what happened to you.

True, I had no power to change it. Maybe you couldn't change it.

True, God hates divorce. And yes, God hates your heartache, regardless of its name.

Check. Check. Check. But more true is the beauty He promises to build from our ashes.

> To comfort *all* who mourn

(That's us folks.)

> and provide for those who grieve *in Zion*—

(Or for those who grieve in your state, grieve in your city, or grieve in your bedroom closet.)

> to bestow on them a crown of beauty
>> instead of ashes,
> the oil of joy
>> instead of mourning,

and a garment of praise
  instead of a spirit of despair.
They will be called *oaks of righteousness*,
  a planting of the LORD
  for the display of his splendor.

(ISAIAH 61:2–3, EMPHASIS ADDED)

I'd opt to be an oak of righteousness if given the opportunity. Sounds much more elegant than being called a pomegranate tree.

Your woeful tales will not be where you linger in the future. Those shadowy spaces may be the starting point, but they will not be the end-all. The end of this bad beginning will come.

Make note: I was really bad at believing this. This is not a book to tell you how successfully I fought the demons that kept knocking. On the contrary. Sometimes it seemed like Halloween every day, and I just kept flinging the door open wide and stuffing fistfuls of Snickers, sour gummies, and M&M's into their sacks. The superstore, super-sized candy packs. Inviting the forces of the underworld to "please, just take more of me."

Honestly, I wondered if I would ever get well. One thing I did know with certainty though: this pain was too excruciating to be wasted. If it was the last thing I did on earth, I was going to recycle the unholy for the holy purposes of heaven. Not because I would will it by the force of my personality or, more hilariously to imagine, transform it by beating it into submission with my stubbornness, but because I remembered a statement issued by Joseph, of amazing-technicolor-coat fame. I intended to claim it for me and my family, just as that long-ago ruler of Egypt had claimed it for his.

After his motley mob of brothers threw him into a pit, sold him off into slavery, and tortured their father by suggesting that wild beasts had torn him apart, Joseph had his chance for revenge handed to him on a silver platter. His response? "As for you, you meant evil against me, but God meant it *for good in order to bring about this present result*, to keep many people alive" (Genesis 50:20 NASB, emphasis added).

Spoken in ancient days, Joseph's pronouncement remains timeless, as the words speak to "good bringing this present result," which I interpret as "good, going on and on and on." To the end of our days.

So, to the end of my days, I want you to know that "this present result" means the following things. You still matter to God even if you don't matter to that one certain person anymore. You still have purpose, even if your platform proves paltry. You aren't invisible, even if your nightmares or the date on your birth certificate tell you otherwise. God doesn't erase us, even if too often our worth seems wanting by society's standards. And although it sucks to endure such griefs, the reclamation of your celestial standing, as beloved, as one of God's own, will be enough to help you draw another breath. It might even make sense one day.

Joseph took a long and winding road before his brothers stood before him, heads hanging in humiliation. He suffered slander and false accusations. Victimized by those holding greater power than he did, Joseph ended up unjustly imprisoned. The irony is not lost—that freedom for Joseph eventually came from a captivity he didn't cause and proved powerless to change. It was in prison that dreams eventually played into his story, as sometimes they do in our own stories.

———

Perhaps trauma from your losses has unleashed a recurring nightmare, delivering the same dose of poison to your soul every night and casting a deathly, bluish tinge over your image when you see it in the mirror. With that distorted reflection looking back at you, you question who you've become as a result. Or did you really know who you were in the first place, before the unthinkable intruded?

Unsolicited negative events prey upon our identities. In our pain, the enemy hisses, "You have been canceled," and we echo it in our ruminations.

And the words ring out.

You are unlovable. Unlovable. Who could love you? Who in this world could ever love you?

Satan relishes our doubts and knows that if we brood on them long enough, it will naturally lead to questioning God's inherent care for us. But the apostle John reminded us that "he [the devil] was a murderer from the beginning, not holding to the truth, for there is no truth in him. When he lies, *he speaks his native language*, for he is a liar and the father of lies" (John 8:44, emphasis added).

How keenly revealing is the description of Satan's native tongue as "Lies." His home country is "Lies." His first words were spoken in "Lies." It's what he turns to when he wants to specifically and skillfully articulate. "Lies" remain his go-to in all circumstances. In a debate tournament, he would run away with the MVP trophy for speaking the most persuasive lies.

I once asked a married couple who were bilingual what language they used as their love language. Was it Spanish or English? "Oh, that's easy," they said. "It's the one we learned when we were children. Our *native language*. We know it best, and the right word comes to us the fastest. That's what we use when we share our most intimate thoughts and affections."

So why do we give the devil an ear into which he can whisper tender lies? How do we allow him access to our intimate longings? Perhaps we don't experience him as the beast he is, but as a skillful litigator who contorts words so we perceive him as our advocate. Satan is an expert at this. He and his demons know the truth better than any of us and use it well. Alfred, Lord Tennyson wrote, "A lie that is a half-truth is the darkest of all lies." This describes our deception perfectly as Satan, the darkest of them all, wraps beguiling lies around the grains of truth until it is too appetizing not to bite them.

We all live our own unique nightmares that differ in the details, but which share strange, sorrowful similarities in the feelings of worth they steal from us. Almost immediately after my childhood-sweetheart-turned-husband walked out the door for the last time, the dreams—those hauntings—rushed right in, anxious to enter through that very same door. Although, now that I think about it, I'm not sure you can call dreams "hauntings" when the main character appears as a noble and beautiful angel.

It was like a movie tape remained jammed in a vintage VHS player that was stuck on a continuous loop. The ending proved utterly predictable.

My mind pushes Rewind. And then Play.

My dream would begin with an image of me floating in an oversized, gilt-edged mirror centered on a wall. The mirror splinters, cracking like a not-frozen-quite-enough pond, and then shatters, with the razor-thin shards instantly disintegrating into crystallized sand. The grains stream down the wall, showering flecks of gold off the gilt-edged frame, and come to rest in a pile on the floor.

My hands instinctively reach up and feel for my face. I also immediately realize that my face is gone and that somehow it . . . or the pieces of it . . . are contained in the glittery dust that lie heaped at the base of that now-vacant, gilt-edged frame.

Enter that noble and beautiful being, an angel, who gently scoops up the pile of crystallized sand, careful to painstakingly pinch and pick up every speck. Momentarily, I feel my breath escape with relief—as I am expecting that she will hand it back to me, but instead, she draws it to her lips and, cupping it to her mouth, blows on the sand. In one startling poof, the dust scatters into a dry sea as far as my eyes can travel. Lost to the hot wind and to a desert of dunes. Forever dispersed. Unable to be gathered together again.

Terrified and realizing that my face is now buried in the miles and miles of sand before me, I throw myself into a frenetic search. Clawing at the mounds and anguished beyond imagination, I am crying in abject terror in fear that I will never be able to be gathered together again. I am undone. Unwound. Untwisted. Stripped clean.

And a phantom voice sobs, "I can't find me anywhere."

That's the point that I would awaken, sweating and snotty and sniffling, "Why would an angel do that to me? Why would she blow me away into a sea of sand? Why can't I find me anywhere?"

The mind can play havoc with the heart when identity is lost. Everything you are, hope to be, or have been is constructed with another life, or another person, as it was with me. When that person leaves, when that career careens off the cliff, when the finances fall through the floor, your identity departs. The movie reel was just the parting gift from your old life as it waved goodbye.

> The mind can play havoc with the heart when identity is lost.

You are unlovable. Unlovable. Who could love you? Who in the world could ever love you?

Certainly not the God of the universe.

In the wake of the nightmare, emotion trumps logic. Irrational thinking plays a deadly game of hopscotch, where Satan chalks the lines and scripts our strategy, scrawling inside the squares drawn on the asphalt.

"You first," he defers, bowing deeply.

Square one.

I read the devilish writing: *I am unloved.*

Square two.

Neon-pink chalk. Really? Pink—my favorite color? *I can't find me.*

Square three.

A giant zero circles the words *I am nothing.*

Hop.

You can't find nothing.

Hop.

Therefore, I must not be.

Leap.

I am not.

And then echoes of "Didn't I tell you? Nothingness is your name."
The accusation hangs in the wind.

Flip to John 8, where the Pharisees engaged Jesus in their own game of playground politics. They jeered, "Who do you think you are? You talk as if you knew Abraham, the big man on campus, but you're just a crazy, snot-nosed kid."

Sounds like the same taunting the deceiver offers us. "You're nothing special. Get over yourself. Who do you think you are?"

Jesus responded with a mic drop of thunderbolt proportions.

"Very truly I tell you," Jesus answered, "before Abraham was born, I am!" (v. 58).

Say, what?

"At this, they picked up stones to stone him" (v. 59).

It's impossible to understand the enormous impact of those two small words "I am" on this crowd of Jewish scholars. This knot of characters knew the sacred Torah by heart and would understand that Jesus was referencing an encounter with Moses, where God, replete in burning-bush garb, identified Himself as the uncreated Creator.

> Moses said to God, "Suppose I go to the Israelites and say to them, 'The God of your fathers has sent me to you,' and they ask me, 'What is his name?' Then what shall I tell them?"
>
> God said to Moses, "I AM WHO I AM. This is what you are to say to the Israelites. 'I AM has sent me to you.'" (Exodus 3:13–14)

"The one who is, who always was, and who is still to come" (Revelation 1:8 NLT).

One who escapes the confines of a clock or a calendar. Boundaryless. Eternally present.

My mind stiffens when I try to wrap it around this idea. It's just so otherworldly. So opposite the sizzling electrical impulses of my brain to constantly accommodate time in every part of my day. A grander concept than my mind can conceive.

Encapsulated in His "I AM" proclamation, Jesus boldly declared His oneness with almighty God, a capital offense to this crowd. (Cue Pharisees picking up big rocks.)

"Believe me," said Jesus, "*I am who I am* long before Abraham was anything" (John 8:58 MSG).

They knew, in that ancient desert place, God's "I AM-ness" announced to a reticent Moses the plan to lead His people from under the oppressive fist of Pharaoh to freedom. Now, Jesus, outrageously declaring the "I AM," was proclaiming His plan to lead from captivity to freedom again. From under the oppressive fist of sin to the freedom of grace. From spiritual bondage to emotional milk and honey. Two "I AMs," eons apart in our earthly domain, and yet instantaneously reverberating in the kingdom of God. God the Father and God the Son timelessly declaring their majesty, simultaneously.

On the heels of this statement clings the reminder that we are made in His likeness, set apart from the rest of creation. Unique. Elevated. Bearing the King's seal. Turn us upside down and you see our soles stickered with the label, "Made by I AM."

And if He is "I AM," and we are fashioned in His image, we can't accept our angst-ridden "I am not." It simply will not reflect the truth. In the volley of Satan's lies about our nothingness, I imagine Jesus crouching down, smoothing and sifting the sand from one hand to another, and then calmly writing two words with His finger over Satan's scrawls. *Imago Dei.* Image of God.

If God is declaring us image bearers, reflectors of His qualities, He stamps us with our value. No other man or thing can name our value. God alone sets our worth by what He sees when He looks at us. His image. His likeness. The words behind the words tumble out of that imagery. "I created you, specifically in my likeness, and I am the I AM. And I will lead you to a new life. From the captivity of *I am not worthy*. From the enslaving *I am not lovable*. From the doubting question hanging on the wind: *Who in the world could possibly love me?*

The heavens must explode in color and music and might when one person grasps this.

And the words sing out, "You are lovable. You are loved. In this whole wide world, it is the Creator of the world who loves you."

Turkey Chili

This is a crowd-pleaser and a nice alternative to beef chili. I like to serve it with lots of toppings, like a good, sharp cheese, fresh cherry tomatoes, pickled jalapeños, sour cream or yogurt, corn chips, and mustard. Yes! I love a good yellow mustard on top of chili.

INGREDIENTS

1 tablespoon olive oil

1 pound ground turkey

1 large onion, coarsely chopped

2 teaspoons salt

1 large green bell pepper, diced

1 large red bell pepper, diced

2 large cloves garlic, finely diced

2 jalapeño peppers, seeded and minced (cut with gloves on) or 1 (4-ounce) can of diced green chilies if you prefer less heat

4 tablespoons tomato paste

1 (28-ounce) can diced tomatoes, including juices

2 tablespoons balsamic vinegar

2 tablespoons chili powder

1 teaspoon sugar

1/2 to 3/4 cup water to thin chili as needed

1 (16-ounce) can red kidney beans, drained

1 (15-ounce) can black beans, drained

DIRECTIONS

1. Heat the olive oil in a large soup pot over medium-high heat. Add the turkey and onions and cook, stirring often. When meat is lightly browned, add the salt, bell peppers, garlic, and jalapeños and cook

until the vegetables are softened. Add the tomato paste, tomatoes, vinegar, chili powder, and sugar. Add water as needed to thin chili.

2. Simmer over low heat at least 1 hour, stirring and tasting for seasonings as you go. Thirty minutes before serving, add the beans and heat through.

Makes 8 servings.

CHAPTER 2

GETTING TO THE ROOT OF THE PROBLEM

*If I had an hour to solve a problem, I'd spend
fifty-five minutes thinking about the problem
and five minutes thinking about solutions.*

—AUTHOR UNKNOWN, BUT SOMETIMES ASCRIBED TO ALBERT EINSTEIN

SOMETIMES IT'S HARD TO PINPOINT *EXACTLY* WHAT'S WRONG. I mean, you know in a larger sense that your world has been turned upside-down, like pink koalas and purple kangaroos should be hopping outside your window, or like big, fat snowflakes should be falling and sticking to the sidewalk on a sweltering summer day.

Somehow, in the throes of trauma, the wildest upendings seem acceptable. As if you've been expecting this theater of the absurd to roll into town. (After all, it was absurd that this hospital bed was now a fixture in the living room along with the strangers and syringes that accompanied it.) But when it really comes down to the minutest details, can you articulate why this loss hurts so deeply? I mean, what *exactly* is the problem?

Jesus knew how to cut through the marshmallowy fluff and reveal the real villain. To pluck the prize at the bottom of the Cracker Jack box. To tease out the splinter instead of just applying a Spiderman Band-Aid over that dark sliver in your thumb. Jesus drilled down to the heart of the matter by calling out the heart of the asker. Like a hot knife gliding through your best chilled cheesecake.

Enter the Pharisees, Scribes, and Sanhedrin. Let the ancient rendition of Truth or Dare begin, in the Gospel of Mark, chapter 7.

"We've got a problem here, Jesus. Your crew of misfits doesn't wash their hands before they eat. They're just pawing at the picnic—passing out loaves and fishes willy-nilly. We do have a rule about that, as you should know—ahem—that is, you *should* know if you really are a prophet." (I mean, these Hebrew Mensa members traveled long, dusty miles from Jerusalem and that's all they've got? That's their best shot?)

Jesus brakes.

"Whoa. Hold on a minute. Aren't you the ones who deny your mother and father support—won't give them a mite—because your money is already cinched up in that 'Devoted to God' pouch? What law could be more devoted to God than 'Honor your father and mother'? You trade the Word of God for your traditions. You trample God's intentions. You say that the problem is handwashing. I say you need a heart-washing."

"For the mouth speaks what the heart is full of" (Matthew 12:34).

That's what you call *exactly* the problem.

And the followers of Jesus were not immune to His laser focus. The earliest teachings of this unorthodox Galilean are exactly that—unorthodox—and feature Him excavating the root problems of surface sins.

Jesus' take on the old laws confounded His listeners. Consider these lessons from Matthew 5:

It's not just that murder is wrong.

It's that unresolved anger toward your brother or sister
is wrong. (vv. 21–22)

It's not just adultery.

It's lust. You know how you looked at that neighbor's
wife? Yep. That one. (vv. 27–30)

Yes. It's divorce all right.

But more than that, underneath divorce, it's like
your hardened heart forces a wife into adultery in future
relationships. It's condemning her. Compromising her.
Casting her aside as collateral damage. (vv. 31–32)

It's not just revenge.

It's stinginess. (vv. 38–40)

Time and again, He calls out the problem underneath the problem.
My friend understood that well. Sitting across from the always
elegant and eternally wise eighty-two-year-old grande dame, I spilled
my guts. Florence Littauer, an accomplished author who had minis-
tered to women for four decades, owned an aura reminiscent of the
tulle-wrapped, very pink, and very glittery Glinda, Oz's famed Good
Witch of the North. And I, a trembling Munchkin, was counting on
her kindness. The imaginary wand she waved would undoubtedly
reflect that kindness, but I was still nervous. Although I had known
her for years (or perhaps *because* I had known her for years), I suspected an edict was forthcoming.

Florence listened, speared the last grape in her chicken salad,
dabbed the corners of her mouth oh so delicately, and with her index
finger wagging, distinctly opined, "Your problem is, you think you
have no value apart from that man."

Ouch. There it was. That was it. Bull's-eye.

You feel worthless.

More specifically, worthless *without him*, a phrase that fits as perfectly as your best little black dress.

That's not a match for your particular situation, you say?

You're probably right. It may not be. Perhaps, as I mentioned earlier, our losses don't resemble each other's in the least little bit.

But see if completing this sentence with *your* words offers clarity. Imagine Florence speaking to you. (Side note: it's helpful to throw in that finger-wagging thing too.)

"You think you have no value apart from _____."

That job? That bank account? That relationship? The success of that superstar child? That home? That car? That title? Those dusty trophies lined up against the window ledge? That perfectly beating heart that pumped you through two elite marathons? Those long-awaited and longed-for Louboutin shoes?

Recalibrating your worth when you lose something temporal you've attached it to proves debilitating. And it doesn't really matter which temporal thing becomes the object of your devotion. All will fail because all are, by definition, fleeting.

Working in a local "stone soup" homeless shelter, I recall a day I manned the clothing trailer. I struck up a conversation with a chatty middle-aged client, as we called the visitors, who took his time poring over the donated jackets hanging on the rack. He pulled out a rather natty plaid coat, propped it up for me to see, and announced, "I wore one like this when I *was* somebody." My soul tore a little for him as I helped him into the sleeves and reflected on the lesson he was teaching me at that very moment, as I was still stuck searching for that old relationship that I'd worn when I *was* somebody. Neither of our garments fit.

These spiritual misappropriations and misplaced self-assessments in light of loss happen in all stratas of society—rich or impoverished, privileged or marginalized. I think the marginalized just may be more honest about it. Hence, natty-plaid-coat-man with the easy confession rolling off his tongue, unknowingly calling out the got-it-all-together volunteer hiding her spiritual snags behind a laminated-lanyard ID tag and rows of hand-me-down coats stuffed into a double-wide.

The movie scene running through my mind cuts to Jesus gathering the children to Him, deliberately corralling the littlest littles and placing them center stage while the disciples, clueless, strut around in the wings, jockeying for position and elbowing each other out of the way, so as to avoid tripping over their extra-long egos.

"Truly I tell you, unless you change and become like little children, you will never enter the kingdom of heaven" (Matthew 18:3).

Well played, Jesus.

The upside-down kingdom of this tough-but-tender Rabbi never fails to flip social structures on their haughty heads.

On the *For the Love* podcast with Jen Hatmaker, Amy Downs, a survivor of the Oklahoma City bombing, was honest about her struggles.[1] She recounted her harrowing and courageous recovery from the ravages of that evil attack.

I was in awe.

She also candidly shared her current battle with identity in the face of loss. An accomplished triathlete, she found herself in a very dark place after a double knee replacement, asking, "Who am I if I am not a cyclist?"

I was in awe again.

Those faulty connections don't die easily, even for the accomplished among us.

But our DNA somehow seems to choreograph the dance we do with our dilemmas—or so I thought that day at lunch. Whatever its root, that was clearly my problem now. My friend and mentor, Florence, nailed it. In a nutshell, I was finding value someplace other than where I was supposed to find it, like looking for love in all the wrong places. (No wonder that song was such a big hit back in the day.)

So there we sat—Florence and I—in that hard reality. My plate full and her plate clean. A fitting metaphor for the heaping plateful of despair I carried with me everywhere.

We were alone in that quiet, post-lunch-rush cafeteria, and her words echoed resoundingly. The syllables bounced off the walls like a pinball game, and I floated into a hypnotic daydream. Magically, glass panels suddenly materialized on the edges of our tabletop and, sliding up and locking into place, encased us in a giant pinball machine. My brain fogged, my eyes glazed over, and I imagined the silver pinball BBs laden with her words—locked, loaded, and launched—pinging off my heart, skipping across her plate, ricocheting off the day-old French rolls, and landing in my lap. For a bizarre few seconds I wondered how long I would be picking out hidden buckshot from my untouched chicken salad and how I would explain this to our waiter.

"My apologies to the chef, sir, but can I send this back? There seems to be a bit of gristle in the chicken."

The empty room seemed cavernous. Sitting opposite each other, our booth seemed cavernous. My heart felt cavernous. The future did too. I was free-falling into a pit, but somehow, that one phrase of awakening caught me before I hit the bottom.

"Your problem is, you think you have no value apart from that man."

It was as if these thirteen words had snagged my sweater on a tree limb poking through the loose dirt of the gravelly cliff and stopped me there to break my death-defying descent. I was hanging upside down and swinging, but alive, and righting myself seemed doable. Difficult. But doable.

That was the truth upon which I would build my recovery. That was the start. In full-on superhero style, Florence swished her cape, unsheathed her verbal machete, and laid bare the root of the problem in one clean swoop.

And that can be the once-deeply-hidden buried treasure upon which you can build your recovery too. *Acknowledging that a new life can exist without that other part of you that is now gone.* This parsing of the problem can start on day one in your season of healing.

> A new life can exist without that other part of you that is now gone.

Whatever the loss. Whatever the grief. This can be your start.

After sitting in that epiphany, I remember asking for advice from a "staff someone" at my church and the long, deafening silence that drowned out his reaction. Sighing, he admitted, "This is really a triage situation and frankly, I don't know how to help you."

In all fairness to this poor guy, he hadn't seen the tsunami coming. Our conversation had started simply enough but quickly picked up speed, like a snowball racing dangerously down a powdery slope. I would start down one trail, only to double back on another while interjecting secondary, less critical issues, like, "My former landlord is suing me," or "Some fire captain just called me and saw smoke billowing out the windows while driving by my house so he just axed down the front door," or "Any chance I could get more coffee?"

By the time I took a breath, he was wound up like a Bavarian pretzel.

It's not that they or he or she or whomever didn't want to help me (at least I don't think so)—it was just so doggone messy. Like that big cauldron of stone soup the volunteers used to concoct at the homeless shelter—every leftover went into that pot, and it proved impossible to know where one ingredient started and the other left off. There were too many to distinguish, so I couldn't name a single one. Like a stone soup on steroids, hence, "stone soup shelter." Now, I guess that I qualified for a "stone soup struggle." Too many problems to name, not knowing where one left off and the next one began.

I decided that there had to be a plan. *Even if no one could provide one.* A road map. Something to point the way, and for me, it made sense to start with Florence's comment: the root of the problem. Square one. I felt a bit lost, but eventually, I'd figure it out.

I drove home from that fateful luncheon, gnawing on that problem over and over again. The new question became, "How? How do I deal with this problem?" How do you spend thirty-five years working diligently to merge, to "become one flesh," only to have to rip it apart? Unlike a clean and sterile amputation, this was a muscle tear, shaggy and shredded, with sinewy fibers raggedly reaching out and nerve cell ganglia writhing in vain looking for their charged counterparts that, apparently, had altogether vanished.

Therein lies the reality of raw grief. It presents as a sawtoothed gash where myriad connections need to be meticulously sewn back together. Traumatic shock, though, doesn't register that at first. Glancing sidelong at the gaping wound, we just want to slather it with some Gorilla Glue, slap it back together like a bologna sandwich, and go play a round of golf. We think we can soldier on, limping away, leaving a trail of blood and assuring the others in our foursome, "I'm okay. I got this. Really, the hemorrhaging should stop by the third tee."

The problem is, the hemorraging doesn't stop. Some of those connections are gluable, but some are minute and take time. Some beg for the skill of an expert and others require plastic surgery, occupational therapy, or a steady hand and a tweezer. Greasing grief's gears takes time, but not just time (unlike the old adage "time heals all wounds"). If the old wound is still gritty with the asphalt you embedded in it when you skidded on that newly tarred street, time will prove insufficient, wanting, an inadequate healer.

Better to clean the wound first with a mixture of therapies. Yes, it will sting. Metaphorically, I scrubbed and sterilized, scraped and squeezed my wounds until I cried "Uncle!" (At which time, and very conveniently, my sweet Uncle Bill demanded we stop and share some strawberry ice cream.) I threw all the persistent pain in and tossed all my old remedies out and mixed up a big ol' heap of healing balm.

I started making a list and checking it twice.

That list began with two new friends, Frank and Honest (as opposed to Frank and Ernest of children's book fame), who carpooled with trusted but long-forgotten old pals—Prayer, Patience, and Self-care. Together with my trusted circle, we marinated in lost practices of scriptural meditations and imagined forgiving those who might ask for forgiveness, and perhaps more dynamically, painfully offering forgiveness to those who would never ask for it.

I must confess that when I couldn't find my appetite, a healthy dose of dark chocolate soothed, and eventually, so did shared meals of comforting food. There were revisions of old perspectives and visions for new ones, healthy and life-affirming distractions, guided self-evaluation, regular showers of grace, pivotal professional resources, and the ever-present, gut-wrenching introspection.

Intentional steps toward physical well-being entered to stay, including long walks in windy places and footsteps falling on crunchy leaves in other spaces. New narratives describing the future filled pretty journal pages. More often, though, the scrawls of my plans found themselves scribbled on neighborhood donut shop napkins or the bottoms and sides of long-emptied to-go coffee cups discovered rolling around under the front seat of the car. All the steps I took toward healing will be explored in the remainder of this book—the ones that helped me process the grief I was convinced would never leave.

And certainly, there will be stories of the *people* who helped me.

Sarah was one of them. Actually, Sarah was the main one. That is common knowledge. Ask anyone who knows me. Under everyone's breath (as they shook their heads at the bone-thin heap of me in the corner) fell the muttered epilogue, "Thank God for Sarah."

Sarah had been my kids' real-life Mary Poppins but without the umbrella. She had landed in America sporting the McGoldrick tartan, a winsome brogue, and a "way with wains" that made me wonder if she actually had been sent over from Central Casting—that movie studio department responsible for filling film roles with stereotypical "types." She arrived on our doorstep before my youngest son was born and when my oldest son was just two. My daughter was eight months old.

My kids don't remember a time when Sarah wasn't there. Neither does anyone else. She just was.

Leaving Scotland behind, she packed away the pain of multiple miscarriages and waved away the smoky tendrils of an incinerated marriage. For thirty-one years, she took the longings of her personal life and flung its lost love fearlessly onto our family. She was my children's second mom, "Gaga" to the adored and arriving grand-littles (the original Lady G), my closest, most loyal confidante and all-around beloved storybook-like figure.

Everyone—I mean everyone—loved "Sadie." I always believed that she could run for mayor of our town and score a landslide victory with no platform other than "beans in every pot and shortbread on every saucer."

Sarah did possess one flaw, however. European football. She cheered appropriately—no wait, I can't actually say that. She cheered *passionately* on the kids' soccer sidelines. No one blinked when she was awarded her long overdue red card (a Scottish rite of passage) and was shown the exit by a referee who, for the record, may have been a little afraid of her. To be clear, though, the Scots take their football *very* seriously, and she grew up alongside Hugh, Andrew, and Jim, brothers who taught her that refs remain fair game until they scamper over the perimeter of the pitch's fence. Made sense to us.

Sarah was simply irresistible.

Her brand? Indescribable.

Her gift? An endless capacity to caretake and care for.

Now, after so many years of her being prominently woven into our lives, I sat beside her, helplessly watching her tumble into a toxic trance as the oncologist droned on and on about the ugly aggressiveness of her cancer. I felt like the warp and weft of the fabric of our family was unraveling at breakneck speed. The disintegrating yarn was piling up in my lap.

We were still freshly grieving our other losses—the teetering budget, the house that was too big and too costly, the mother with declining energy and health, and, most of all, the absence of the father and husband who we couldn't imagine not cherishing his role, as difficult as that might have been at times. When the kids and I drove our old faithful family dog to the vet to be "put down," no one said a word. It just seemed like we were always saying goodbye to someone or something. And Sarah and her Scottish sensibilities had kept us upright and marching forward.

This can't be happening, Lord.

The surgeon had "forgotten" to tell Sarah about her lab results and subsequent dire diagnosis, and in his words, Sarah had "fallen through the cracks." Now, another specialist sitting in front of us seemed to be part of a Tag Team Terrible that was making sure that she couldn't crawl out of those cracks. She never deserved to "fall through the cracks." No human deserves such a placement. Especially one who clearly had been blindsided, kidnapped, and deposited in the farthest, most frightening margins of life, all in the span of eight hours.

With the skill of a trained assassin, and the utter absence of even a drop of compassion, this doctor described a swift and angry end.

Not unlike Florence, the clinician before us also wielded a sharp tool. But when Florence culled out truths that were painful to reveal, she did so with a heart of compassion. Conversely, this assassin (perhaps *really* sent over from Central Casting) appeared unfeeling and dispassionate, cruelly swirling a virtual scalpel in that small, white-walled examination room—excising hope and, frankly, cutting out all acknowledgment of human value or sacred standing. She almost appeared to relish her words.

She was honest, and I would agree that that's important, but at the same time, her words rang out heartless and hardened and heinous.

Leading Sarah by the hand, it was all I could do to navigate our way to the bank of elevators where I texted the wains—the ones whose bottoms had been powdered by the hands that I now held—to meet us at our little house on Wilson Street.

Jesus. A man acquainted with grief. How I clung to that familiar description on this day before Christmas—famished for a faith full enough to embrace it, but at the same time, hating it, and wanting to reject it more. Give me a second opinion, another description . . .

Healer.

Living Water.

The Balm of Gilead.

Anything but being chummy with grief.

But on that December 24, we tried, the kids and I. We summoned our fragile faith, wrapped our arms around our friend, and wept. Together. Deeply. As a family should. Or would. Or tries to clumsily, at times like these.

And the damage done by this brutal honesty without hope or love? This was the problem we attacked. This was the problem underneath that *other* problem, the one we could do nothing to change.

Another picture of Jesus began to emerge.

The shepherd leaving the ninety-nine to seek *the one* (Matthew 18:12).

The one who may be wounded by the elements of a hostile environment, but esteemed nonetheless.

The one still worth seeking, "in spite of."

The one, like *you*, in your grief today. He'll always search for *the one*. He'll *always* search for you.

That day, I saw Sarah as *the one* and I knew that He did too. What would *that* Shepherd do?

Then I saw her. *The one* at the well. Jacob's well.

The one who faced the searing heat of the sun's position high in the sky, to avoid the searing heat of rejection from her critics, unaware of the "Someone" waiting by the well to change her life forever. Her humanity looked a bit tattered, what with so many men in and out of her life who, with every departure, tore off fluffy pieces of her like pink cotton candy at a carnival.

The woman at the well. The one whom the disciple John described as hiding the "too long a list" of disappointing partners. Parched. Lonely. Rejected. Despised. Abandoned. Isolated. Tossed aside. Tired to the bone. A mouth that had tasted only bitterness in the face of loss.

And Jesus spoke an uncomfortable truth to her, gingerly peeling back the layers. John 4 showcases a difficult honesty but one bundled in a gentle kindness.

He told her, "Go, call your husband and come back."

"I have no husband," she replied.

Jesus said to her, "You are right when you say you have no husband. The fact is, you have had five husbands, and the man you

now have is not your husband. What you have just said is quite
true." (vv. 16–18)

And yet, to this *one*, clearly broken, Jesus identifies Himself as
the Messiah and chooses *her*—a Samaritan woman steeped in despair
and discrimination—to announce His identity. What crazed casting
agent thought that was a good idea?

> The woman said, "I know that Messiah" (called Christ) "is com-
> ing. When he comes, he will explain everything to us."
>   Then Jesus declared, "I, the one speaking to you—I am he."
> (vv. 25–26)

An unlikely herald. The unlikeliest of *ones,* proclaiming an
unlikely Messiah in an unlikely setting to an unlikely people.

He selects *the one.*

You can't make this stuff up.

And the stories of more women continue. Despairing women in
dark days. Does any of it feel familiar?

Mark 5:21–34 illuminates the bleeding woman who touched
Jesus' cloak.

Imagine her despair as she grieves the loss of her health, her femi-
ninity, and likely, her fertility. Physically sick. Anemic. Exhausted.
Dirty. Untouchable and untouched. Depleted. Desperate. Unwanted.
Overlooked.

Fallen through the cracks.

Yet, Jesus stops in His tracks. He acknowledges her.

When skirting the edges and crowded by others appearing much
more important than you, He picks you out of the crowd. He sees the
unseen and those of us who have felt unseen.

He sees *the one.*

John 20:1–18 describes Mary at the garden tomb. Grieving the violent death of her teacher. Her best friend. No doubt traumatized by its brutality.

And what does He do? He speaks in a way so intimate as to reveal His nature and expose their relationship.

"Mary."

With a single word, recognition sparks.

He speaks to *the one.*

What might God do in our despair? God not only doesn't disparage the despairing, He repurposes them in mighty ways. Even me. Even you. I know. It's hard to swallow.

Their lessons are recorded for a reason, though, written in a time and a culture when women possessed zero value. Or slide to the left on the number line and let's call it what it is: negative value. These narratives' presence in the holy passages speak volumes before you read one word. Jesus lifts women

> God not only doesn't disparage the despairing, He repurposes them in mighty ways.

at every opportunity, but especially in their grief. These stories teach us about His care through the power of gentle but direct honesty, His inclusiveness to a gender rarely included in anything, and the lingering lilt of the name He calls you.

———

And finally, about that theater of the absurd mentioned in the opening of this chapter.

It was Sarah who required those strangers and syringes. It was Sarah who we tried to keep snug in her hospital bed in the living room at the little house on Wilson Street. And it was Sarah who was surrounded by those who loved her with the depth reserved for the most honored among us. Encircled by her Scottish family, the family she was born to, and us, the family she chose, we collectively became stand-ins for the woman who didn't have the strength to reach for His cloak on her own.

On Sundays, the trio of oldest grandchildren (three-year-olds) stood on the rock-faced hearth that elevated them just enough to see Sarah's face in that oversized bed. With childlike abandon, they serenaded her with sweet and simple hymns in the full voices of unselfconscious toddlers.

They kept time with their little hands, stomped their feet at all the right parts, blessing her soul and admonishing all of us to keep singing, even as evening drew near.

The evening had come. Or Sarah's evening had come.

It is true that she was not healed of her cancer. That is a hard thing for some of us to admit, as if God could not be God if He didn't answer my prayers the way I wanted. I get that. My heart understands without judgment.

My true expectation, though, lies in a healing beyond what we can touch and taste.

When Irene, one of her sisters, whispered, "Fly high, hen," and Sarah took her last breath, we believed that hope, healing, and heart had been restored, obviously in a different dimension.

At that time, I wrote on Instagram,

Dear Sarah, Life is not as much fun without you. Come home now, please.

In truth, Sarah is the one who is home, and ironically I am the one displaced. I long for eternity where boundaries of time and space break and the pain of our losses are neither contained or counted anymore.

I don't have all the answers, but those are the words that anchor me in the storms. My belief. My longing. And when I bristle a bit thinking that Sarah should never have died so soon and how much she would love all these grandbabies, I thank God for keeping my heart soft so that I can feel others' pain, and I read this again.

I long for eternity where boundaries of time and space break and the pain of our losses are neither contained or counted anymore.

I don't doubt my love for Jesus or my faith. I just thank God for reminding me of my humanity so that I could stay "squishy" and hurt for people afresh.

I couldn't control the date of Sarah's passing. But I could contribute to the setting in which she passed. Sarah died knowing she was so important to us. So esteemed by us. So adored by the Father. Never would she fall between the cracks in His eyes.

The honesty of the situation proved excruciatingly painful. Earthly events can be excruciating. Yes. I said it—even for those who love Jesus or believe in a just God. That's okay. That's how He made us. Pain acutely reminds us that we are alive.

There was no earthly healing, but the sacred and the valuable had been welcomed back into that space, and none of us will ever forget that moment, and none of us will ever forget her name. It hovers in the room when a baby's bottom is powdered, when the teakettle whistles, or the strains of "Bless the Lord" fill the church.

How I wish I could thank Florence again, although she, too, has passed and been restored to a fullness reserved for eternity. I would tell her how her words accompanied me through deep waters and reminded me that there is a purpose behind what lies on the surface. That understanding the problem has the potential to remake us—to put the broken pieces of our life stories back together in a way that cherishes the cracks and allows the imperfections to love ourselves and others well. As the wounds in Jesus' hands reassure us of a resurrected life, the wounds of our griefs can reassure us of a heart to love ourselves and others as He did. A new life "on earth as it is in heaven" . . . in the kingdom of God that is the here and now.

Chicken Salad à la Florence

I've made this a zillion times for ladies' luncheons and showers. It's an all-purpose, all-around, always good go-to. Nothing overly fancy but reliably down-to-earth and relatively inexpensive, like the '72 VW bug I drove in college.

Make this the night or day before you plan on serving it. Another plus.

SALAD

4 chicken breasts, poached or roasted, cut into bite-size pieces

2 cups seedless green or red grapes, halved (I like using half red and half green)

1 (11-ounce) can mandarin oranges, drained with juice reserved

1 whole fresh pineapple, peeled and cut into bite-size pieces

1 cup blanched almonds, slightly toasted*

4 ribs celery, chopped

2 cups dry pasta, cooked al dente (I prefer bow-tie pasta)

10 dried apricots, quartered (optional)

1 to 2 teaspoons fine salt

DRESSING

2/3 cup high-quality mayonnaise

1 to 2 tablespoons chicken broth

1 to 2 tablespoons mandarin orange juice (as reserved above)

DIRECTIONS

1. Combine the chicken, grapes, mandarin oranges, pineapple, almonds, celery, pasta, and optional apricots in a large serving bowl and gently toss.
2. To prepare the dressing, combine the mayonnaise, chicken broth, and reserved juice from the mandarin oranges. Add the dressing to the salad and toss to coat. Add the salt and toss again. Refrigerate until time to serve. Serve over butter lettuce or as-is on a buffet.

Makes 10 servings.

Cook's note: Put blanched almonds on a baking sheet and into a preheated 350-degree oven for 6 to 8 minutes. Check regularly after 4 minutes, as they can go from golden to burned rather quickly. Let cool before using.

CHAPTER 3

IS REDEMPTION EVEN A REAL THING?

You, LORD, took up my case;
you redeemed my life.
—LAMENTATIONS 3:58

I GREW UP IN A FAMILY OF SEVEN KIDS. MAYBE THAT'S WHY, WHEN I look back at those black-and-white, scallop-edged pictures of myself, I always looked a little half-put-together. My hair skewed somewhat scraggly at the ends, and for some reason, my pants seemed to be worn a bit too high. Maybe hand-me-downs had something to do with it, and also the fact that I'd rather be playing baseball with Mikey Whipple up the street.

Yep. It could be chaotic, what with one of us always dragging home a neighbor kid for Monday meatloaf or Saturday spaghetti or sneaking in a pregnant stray calico who invariably gave birth to a litter of feral kittens in a cardboard box under our dining room table.

Number one, my mom was creative; number two, she bought a lot of groceries. Those two facts gave us access to something that my seven-year-old self found mysteriously compelling: books of super-market Blue Chip Stamps.

One of her clever ways to keep us occupied was to load us up and stuff us into the gold-and-white Chevrolet station wagon (with no seat belts "way back when") and head to the Blue Chip Redemption Center. Jostling around on the inside of the car, between the seats of the Chevy, she'd toss us each a stamp book or three. We would file in with our own treasure trove of these books and spend what seemed like hours poring over the merchandise in the showroom, studying carefully what our stack of books might buy.

It seemed like such an unfair trade. Mind you, we had no concept of what it cost to get these reams of stamps. We only knew that if the supermarket's shopping cart was full enough, the stamps would fly out of the machine next to the checker's cash register and triple fold over on the counter, spilling onto the linoleum-checkered floor. Appeared free to me.

It seemed crazy. We had these mounds of, well, basically paper, and we could hand them over for a toaster or a stereo or even a set of golf clubs. Of course, I had no idea why we would want the golf clubs. My family fell far from the cashmere-cardigan-country club set. And it's terrifying to think of what the unruly gang of us might do with a nine iron. It just seemed like a top-of-the-line "get" back then and the peak of the mountain as far as prizes went. Something you should aspire to own because of how indulgent it was.

Somehow, I felt in my child's mind that we were pulling a fast one on those poor suckers working in the showroom.

"You mean, Mom, I could simply walk in with these worthless books, filled with crookedly placed stamps licked by us [another way to keep us busy and that made our tongues feel very dry and very thick, very much like a nubby terry-cloth beach towel], hand them over to the clerk in the showroom, and then we could load something really good into the station wagon?"

Magic.

I always craned my neck out the back window of the station

wagon as we pulled away, half-expecting to see a nimble, high-heeled, shirtwaist-dressed June-Cleaver-wannabe or a middle-aged man with horn-rimmed glasses chasing after us in the getaway car.

So on one rainy Sunday, when I heard the pastor explain that God wouldn't waste our pain, that He wanted to redeem our losses—including my nobody-famous-just-little-ol'-me-garden-variety worthlessness (isn't it funny that somehow I thought there was a hierarchy of loss and mine would certainly be at the bottom of the heap—the "lowest value" loss?)—that He would trade it in for something good, suddenly the golf clubs made sense.

Excessive. Extravagant. Indulgent.

Here I stood before Him, the Creator of the universe, like the little girl who wore her pants just too darn high, clinging to books of crookedly placed stamps, moistened not by dry, nubby tongues but by countless tears and pasted into a book that I held pressed to my chest. Stamps that represented not grocery store baskets full of Cheerios and Cheetos, bananas and bacon, but costlier items named rejection, abandonment, fear, shame, embarrassment, worthlessness, and grief. I had to learn to loosen my grip, open my hands, and reach toward Him with a whispered, "Please redeem these, Sir. Yes. For something good."

More impactfully, though, I had this vision of Satan craning his neck, checking to see if I believed that this redemption was real, and in particular, real for "nobody-famous, garden-variety-worthless, just-little-ol'-me." But this time, unlike the groceries, I did have a concept of the price tag. Something about the All-Powerful One carrying a cross with every one of my aforementioned costlier labels seared to His soul.

It was the ultimate life lesson in understanding *redemption*—that fancy word bandied about in Sunday school without much of an explanation of what it was. A big word with an even bigger meaning, and I'm not sure we embrace it until we want to unload some dreadfully bulky baggage later in life. Like Mrs. Winchell, my fifth-grade Sunday school teacher at the Baptist church on the corner, who explained her brain surgery and her hope in practically the same breath.

Mrs. Winchell was one of those people in your life who is impossible to fully appreciate until you've gotten a few decades of adulting under your belt. Which, in a way, was part of her beauty because the memory of her faith is a gift that keeps on giving—in a good way.

I want to point this out, because I am sure there are devoted fifth-grade teachers who show up every week and leave, wondering if they've made any impact at all. But, here, all these years later, I can visualize the profile she drew on the blackboard in our classroom off the fellowship hall, showing us how her tumor was going to be cut out of her head. Sound gruesome? No. What I recall is the tone of her voice as she announced to her Sunday ducklings that she would be back, and that she was going to be wearing some fantastic turbans to cover her bald head.

I can't imagine that she wasn't afraid, but I only remember her steady and uplifting presence, and my eyes grew as wide as saucers with her raw explanations. I think, too, it was the first time I realized that it was okay to talk about things in church that "weren't so pretty" (I mean, isn't that the idea?) and that sometimes God's faithful were going to be drawing pictures on the blackboard with shaky hands.

Years later, long after Mrs. W's death from her brain tumor, when I saw her son around our high school campus, I silently wondered if he knew how much his mom had been prized, and if he still carried a little place inside of him filled with broken glass for missing her. Again, I think her transparency pricked in me a desire to stay squishy when it comes to the pain of others. To be mindful of pain and not to be afraid to talk to people about it. I didn't know how to unpack that then, but later in life, when I wondered if there was hope for a better future for me, memories of her came flooding back. I supposed that this was a gift of redemption from her, still at work.

I have come to suspect that healing starts with this: believing that redemption is possible. That this bad thing—and what Mrs. Winchell endured *was* a very bad thing—can be swapped for something good. That your story doesn't end here and in this way. The idea that good can come out of bad promises power and possibilities beyond what might seem reasonable, even beyond our individual lifetimes, as in the case of Mrs. Winchell.

> I have come to suspect that healing starts with this: believing that redemption is possible.

I would go as far as to say that nothing matters if you don't believe redemption is really a thing and that it's really a thing *for you*. You can take all the steps and enlist all the strategies in the world, but if you don't hold hope in redemption, those processes will remain poor companions for what will be a hard journey.

If you doubt, I can't say that I blame you. Simply stated, sometimes we can't possibly imagine how anything good or pure or honorable or worthwhile can come out of the ways of God. There. I said it. Sometimes I just can't see it.

God tends not to fix things the way we would—or the way we think He should. Have you noticed His alternate routes? It started with His entrance to earth that first Christmas morning.

Two words.

Baby.

Redeemer.

That's the craziest coupling I've ever seen. Seems to me that *Baby*

Redeemer is a magnificent oxymoron. At once helpless and holy. Does anyone else see the ridiculousness of that?

When referring to the upheaval of a newborn's arrival, it was clear why my mom used to say, "What a difference seven pounds makes in a household." Babies are dependent, defenseless, and take loads of work 24-7. The thought that mankind's redeeming Savior would be delivered in this kind of packaging strikes me as ludicrous and ingenious all at the same time.

Count it as our initiation into this new kingdom-speak that makes so little sense to us. A dynamic where God arrives on the scene and immediately begins doing things exactly the opposite way of what seems right, logical, or sensible. Jesus' birth announcement might just as well have read, "Expect the unexpected," or "Surprise! He's arrived and you aren't gonna believe what's next," accompanied by a black-and-white, scallop-edged picture of the conquering hero swaddled in a stone feeding trough, which just hours before had belonged to the donkey braying in the background.

In a funny sort of way, it reminds me of ninth-grade English class. I recall dreading the start to such a dusty and outdated assignment as reading *Les Misérables*. I also recall, though, being swept away by the pages of Jean Valjean's redemptive transformation born when the gracious priest gives him the candlesticks in the presence of Valjean's relentless accuser. The gift of grace, by definition unasked for and undeserved, and given freely from the innocent one to the one who is truly guilty—in full view of the foiled antagonist. I was impressed by the priest, obviously, but more impressed with author Victor Hugo and how he orchestrated that beautiful, moving, and unexpected twist with such literary mastery. I never would have thought of that. We mere mortals cry, "Oh, to be able to write like that!"

It's an inadequate analogy for understanding that God's ways are not our ways, but maybe it gets one thinking along those lines. God, as the Author of all, writing the twist that our finite minds could not pen on our own. The angels must surely cry, "Oh, to be able to write like that!"

If this initiation into God's ways gives you pause, you aren't alone. Read the parable below, understanding that Jesus taught in relatively simple stories because the concepts were just so wild. And remember, the disciples got after-hours tutoring to help them grasp the stories more fully. Wouldn't we all have loved to be a fly on those walls?

> This is what the kingdom of God is like. A man scatters seed on the ground. Night and day, whether he sleeps or gets up, the seed sprouts and grows, *though he does not know how.* All by itself the soil produces grain—first the stalk, then the head, then the full kernel in the head. As soon as the grain is ripe, he puts the sickle to it, because the harvest has come. (Mark 4:26–29, emphasis added)

The scattered seeds remind me of my ranunculus, the perpetual stars of my springtime garden.

Current status: buried completely.

Totally invisible. Covered in dirt. Shrouded in soil. Washed by rain. Incubated by stormy skies.

No promise of pretty.

Yet.

Ranunculus, the blossoms I nicknamed the Sugar Plum Fairy of the flower world, with their tissue-paper tutus dancing so delicately in any arrangement they grace. Saturated with color. Expensive to buy. Dripping in delicacy. Fragile. Desirable and desired.

But have you ever seen the seed—aka the tuber—from which they start? Brown. Twisted. Gnarled. A seed fallen from grace if ever there was one.

I had planted some tubers, and when I walked by the patch of dirt holding them, I thought, *Hmm. Looks like a patch of dirt to me.*

And every day, when I looked into the mirror in my deep days of grieving, sizing up my reflection and still reeling from rejection, I thought, *Hmm. Looks like a patch of dirt to me.*

And yet, "night and day, whether he sleeps or gets up, *the seed sprouts and grows, though he does not know how*" (v. 27, emphasis added).

After a while—and after walking by many times and thinking, *Hmmm. Looks like a patch of dirt to me*—I will spy shoots of fresh chartreuse sprouts, strong necks of sturdy stems, and then layers of fantastic fuschia folds and bright, taxi-cab-yellow buds. As if nature had been playing a game of hide-and-seek and at last had called, "Come out, come out, wherever you are."

I never see the in-between. I never do. I never will. Only the beginning, when the initial work of planting the ugly takes place—and the reward, when the pretty is posied (florist-speak for gathering the bouquet).

This redemption thing doesn't happen because we chant some magic words and hold onto some fairy-tale notion that progress will sprout as in Jack and the Beanstalk, sowing enchanted seeds. It will take place when you open yourself up—meaning, when you give mental assent and space—to the possibility that the One who made you and knows you best is doing transformative work in and through your pain—work that for many days you cannot see.

That though there have been failures, and disappointments, and abandonments, just as Israel had repeatedly demonstrated, God will not turn His back on you. He will esteem you anew.

> God will remain faithful. He will rename you out of your sorrowful identity.

God will remain faithful. He will rename you out of your sorrowful identity. He will rejoice over you as He did with Israel despite her brokenness.

The key is, you likely cannot see that happening in your little patch of dirt. No, ma'am. No, sir.

My therapist used to say it in a different way. In response to my ever-present and stubborn feelings of worthlessness and my musings as to whether God would grow impatient with my lack of progress, she would lean forward in her chair, grab her dog-eared Bible, fan through the translucent paper pages, park her index finger in a high-lighted passage, lock eyes with mine, and read this aloud:

> No longer will they call you Deserted,
> or name your land Desolate.
> But you will be called Hephzibah. (Isaiah 62:4)

"Hep-zi-*what*? I don't know if I want to be called that."
I couldn't quite envision that written on my venti to-go cup.
"Carole, hold on. That means, 'God's Delight.' And listen to this":

> You will be called Hephzibah,
> and your land Beulah;
> for the LORD will take delight in you,
> and your land will be married. (v. 4)

"Your land will be married—huh?"
Apparently an ancient way of saying that my land will be like Party Central (my interpretation).
My therapist continued,

> As a bridegroom rejoices over his bride,
> so will your God rejoice over you. (v. 5)

Now you're talking.
I have to admit. That last line got me. I had recently married off

three children, and I rejoiced in the fulfilled longings and joy that I saw in each of the bridegrooms' eyes when his bride walked down the aisle. Always my favorite moment. Like they'd just won the lottery and the ultimate prize stood before them swathed in silk and glistening in glitter.

"That's how God looks at you, Carole."

Girl, come out. Come out. Wherever you are.

With that word picture, I started to believe, a teeny-tiny fraction, that God saw me as a partner, as if we had a future together, with promise and potential and yes, even celebration. A redeemed woman. Esteemed. Delightful. From discarded to delighted in. From rejected to redeemed.

I sucked in air as her words sunk in.

"Do you see that, Carole? Do you get that, Carole?"

"Please," I said, sitting up a bit straighter in my chair. "Call me Hephzibah."

> Israel, put your hope in the LORD,
> for with the LORD is unfailing love
> and with him is full redemption. (Psalm 130:7)

Saturday Spaghetti

*Vegan with a gluten-free twist: spaghetti
squash instead of pasta*

Spaghetti sauce slowly simmering on a Saturday makes you feel like a real cook because of the fragrance wafting through your house. When friends walk through the door, you can grab a wooden spoon and start stirring, spouting Italian phrases like, *"Bene bene, molto bene."*

When my grandson, Jett, said he wanted to be a chef, this is the first sauce we made together. You can use it in so many ways and it freezes well. It is a vegan recipe, but you can add ground beef, turkey, or sausage to make it your way.

INGREDIENTS

1 large spaghetti squash

4 tablespoons olive oil, divided

1 sweet onion, diced

3 carrots, diced

3 cloves garlic, minced

1 ½ teaspoons Italian seasoning

1 teaspoon sugar

2 teaspoons salt

Freshly ground black pepper to taste

1 (28-ounce) can crushed tomatoes*

Parmigiano Reggiano cheese (optional)

DIRECTIONS

1. Preheat the oven to 400 degrees.

2. Prepare the squash by cutting it in half and removing the seeds with an ice cream scoop. Brush the cut sides of the squash with 2 table-spoons of the olive oil and place the halves, cut side up, on a baking sheet. Roast for 40 minutes until easily pierced with a fork. Let cool.

3. Heat the remaining 2 tablespoons of olive oil in a large sauté pan or soup pot over medium heat until the oil shimmers. Add the onions and carrots and cook 10 minutes over medium-low heat until the onions are translucent and the carrots are softened a bit. Lower the heat and add the garlic, stirring so it does not burn. Sauté 2 minutes more, adding the Italian seasoning, sugar, salt, and pepper and stir-ring to combine. Add the tomatoes with their juices and simmer for 30 minutes.

4. While the sauce is simmering, shred the squash with a fork. It will pull away in spaghetti-like tendrils. Cover the squash with plastic wrap and refrigerate until the sauce is done. To serve, cut the squash halves into 4 to 6 servings, top with the sauce, and sprinkle with grated Parmigiano Reggiano if using.

Makes 4 to 6 servings.

Cook's note: San Marzano brand is best. You can also use a can of whole peeled tomatoes and just break them up as you cook them.

CHAPTER 4

STAND IN YOUR PAIN

I, more and more in my life, have discovered that the gifts
of life are often hidden in the places that most hurt.
—Henri Nouwen

WHEN I READ THE ABOVE WORDS FROM HENRI NOUWEN, I
thought, *Uh Henri . . . any other option?* How's that for a spiritually
mature response?

Hiding your pain is not the way of Jesus.

I hate that truth. And generally speaking, most Christians in pain
hate that truth. Not the way we want to roll. No, thank you. We'll
just take a bed, a blanket, and some beefy blackout curtains, please.

I was more than happy to bury the two of us (my shattered soul
and me) in a room with thick pull-down shades and fluffy down
duvets. Pile me under that mess and let me be.

Not unlike the princess and the pea, though, there remained a bit
of a rub lurking under all those metaphoric mattresses. You see, I had
a problem.

His name was Tommy.

Tommy is my son-in-law and a therapist who understood the error
of those ways.

I hope you have a problem like Tommy.

The first official day of my separation, I nearly tripped over a well-loved copy of theologian Henri Nouwen's *Life of the Beloved* set outside my bedroom door, steps away from my cocoon of a hiding place. Next to it was propped a CD labeled "Worship," stark in its black Sharpie lettering, familiar hand, and inferred intent. Tommy's fingerprints were all over it. A good one-two punch in his therapist's toolbox.

But "Worship"?

Really?

I'm supposed to worship? *Now?*

I had barely hung up from a call where a kindly, but direct, message lingered.

"Thanks, but we won't be needing your contract services anymore. We'll be going in-house from now on. Budgetary issues, unfortunately. Your final paycheck will go in the mail tomorrow."

That, together with the abrupt departure of my husband, hit squarely below the belt. I felt depleted. To put it mildly.

The tiny tome's title alone—*Life of the Beloved*—wrecked me. Clearly, I was no one's "beloved," and I certainly could not begin to grasp Nouwen's proposal that I was "God's beloved."

As for that CD, I could barely mouth the lyrics to anything past the first song. I found myself prostrate on the cream-colored carpet in my closet, rummaging under my tennies, wishing I could magically unearth a pit of sooty ashes to dust on top of my head and clothes that I could rend more easily than the gray sweats I never intended to take off.

Suddenly, it struck me that this was, in fact, the perfect posture for worship. Exactly what the doctor, Tommy, and the Father he knew so well had ordered.

"When I [Ezekiel] saw all this, I fell to my knees, my face to the ground" (Ezekiel 1:28 MSG).

Nothing like a little Old Testament, flat-on-your-face, got-nothing-left adoration.

Tommy didn't give that book to me because he thought I would go to sleep at night giggling, with visions of sugarplums dancing in my head, or contentedly counting sheep frolicking over a paddock gate in Yorkshire. He knew it was more likely to provoke a foreboding dark night of the soul, the dreaded come-to-Jesus introspective that most of us work to avoid at all costs.

I dutifully read the Nouwen book with sad resignation, though, and underlined the concept of standing in my pain, drinking it in deeply as it promised to produce things that would draw me close to the heart of Jesus (my interpretation of Nouwen's words). I would breathe in huge gulps and croak, "Okay. If that's the deal, then open the floodgates and let's get this over with."

I begged the Father to let each nerve ending sizzle, and I silently cursed every single one when they did.

Had I lost the concept that hard can be good? Would I shy away from difficult for me and for my children? Tommy recognized our human tendency to steer clear of pain and invited me into it nonetheless. It reminded me of Proverbs, where Wisdom suggests that there is far greater value in a companion bringing the tough truths of life than showing up with Turkish Delight to coat our tongues with sugary substitutes.

> Wounds from a friend can be trusted,
> but an enemy multiplies kisses. (Proverbs 27:6)

Tommy loved me that much.

It moves me to tears to this very day.

Let's be real though. You don't have to *like* the trauma. Sometimes I think, as Christians, we're expected to snuggle up next to it, take our licks, and then, giddy like the sheepdog I once owned, roll around in the grass ecstatically, as my puppy would do following his dreaded flea bath. That somehow such ecstasy will elevate us to sainthood.

That's weird. No one should like loss. You can accept it. You can respect the change it's ushered into your world. You can even embrace it and choose to apply the lessons learned, using the healing to help others. But no one is saying that you should like it.

> Stand in your pain as opposed to side-stepping it.

I simply say stand in your pain as opposed to sidestepping it.

"Going a little farther, he fell with his face to the ground and prayed, 'My Father, if it is possible, may this cup be taken from me'" (Matthew 26:39).

Jesus, in this familiar verse, asked for the cup of suffering to pass. Does its familiarity blind us to the fact that it's pretty clear it wasn't His preference? Thank God that the Gospels recorded these words for us, so in our wavering uncertainty about the value of pain and our aversion to its discomfort, we could find a friend and an ally in Him.

It brings to mind one of my favorite C. S. Lewis quotes: "Friendship is born at that moment one person says to another, 'What! You too? I thought I was the only one.'"[1]

I recall hearing the late author-speaker Marilyn Heavilin, a woman dearly acquainted with loss, rail against her own expertise. Sitting in the audience and touched by her transparent lament over the unimaginable loss of three children, I heard her honestly challenge God, admitting that she didn't want to be that person whose experience made her an expert on grief. Her openness disarmed me. Childlike vulnerability reigned.

It was a heart-wrenching, intimate ask to have her cup pass as well.

Me? I thought back to a long-ago vacation in Greece where the after-dinner entertainers hurled cups . . . and plates . . . and glasses . . . into the fireplace and smashed them to smithereens. With abandon and a certain artistic flair, I might add.

It was great.

So therapeutic.

Yeah. That's what I want to do with my "cup."

I think the Greeks were onto something when they incorporated that smashing-plates tradition into mourning—along with tzatziki, which I regularly smear on everything. I regret to admit that I solidly align with the hot-blooded Mediterraneans here, more than my ice-in-their-veins Scandinavian tribe, whose emotional rants might include, "Ouuu. Hmmm. Ja. Well. Doncha know. Pass the lutefisk, please." (I truly do love my Scandinavian lineage, and they outdid themselves with the krumkake and spritz butter cookies to vastly make up for the pickled herring nonsense.)

Henri Nouwen said, "Suffering is a period in your life in which true faith can emerge, a naked faith, a faith that comes to life in the midst of great pain . . . and when you dare to stand in your suffering, your life will bear fruit in ways that are far beyond your own predictions or understanding."[2]

In other words, if you want a crop, you've got to till the soil.

While you're standing, can you also speak about what happened to you? Acknowledging loss tangibly was, for me, a key that unlocked the door to the grief. By tangibly, I mean I needed to audibly *say* it, and usually to write it down. Before my ability to match language with feelings, I struggled with all kinds of extreme emotions, runaways recklessly racing laps around my heart, which dangerously sped up to keep pace. The result proved as effective as a poorly cut key getting jammed into a lock. The more I forced it, the more it stuck and the less likely it would ever turn to open anything. And my heart? Well, it finally just pooped out—hence the state-of-the-art pacemaker-defibrillator-thingamajig that lies nestled under a shiny scar on my chest.

I started noticing, though, that simple questions could pierce tucked-away tensions and drain away some of the poison. I learned to sit in these questions, feeling like I had become a professional ponderer. My responses sometimes made it to journals, but mostly, as I mentioned before, onto those rolling-around-on-the-floorboard to-go coffee cups.

Words seemed to arrive spontaneously while I was driving, often listening to music, which probably triggered some nugget in my subconscious. I was the one you passed on the road, pulled off to the shoulder with my hazard lights flashing, writing furiously on the cardboard cup from the last drive-through burger joint. Sophisticated it was not.

Reflect on questions like these—and amend them to suit your circumstances.

- How did it feel the first time a friend lightly touched your arm and said, "I'm so sorry"?
- Did your heart ache when you spoke aloud the word *gone*?
- Were you able to grasp and identify the helplessness that swirled when the surgeon delivered the word *inoperable*?

While silence can be golden, it can sometimes weigh us down; we need words to liberate us from the chains of denial. As a regular eleven o'clock ritual, I learned to recite, "It's not what I am, but it's what happened to me."

I recall an early therapy session when I launched into a blurry monologue of jumbled emotions. My therapist listened intently and without interruption—always amazing what a basic-but-effective therapeutic tool that remains. No doubt assessing the accompanying anxious hand-wringing, he nodded thoughtfully, tracking my tears, and after my soliloquy, posed the million-dollar question: "How does that make you feel? I mean—all that you described—how does that make you feel?"

Such a simple question, right?

I sat there, like a deer in the headlights, in stunned silence.

"I don't know. I suppose I never stopped to wonder about that."

All at once, it seemed the swirling sand sifted through the hourglass and the answer was lying on top of the pile's peak. It lay there, a wisp of white paper, waiting to be picked up.

"Abandoned."

That's how I felt.

That one word gave order to a Scrabble board full of formerly disjointed square tiles. It was as if I'd stumbled upon a triple word score and managed to use all seven letters at the same time. Bingo! I picked up fifty points and, more importantly, the notion that maybe I could finish this game after all.

Yes. That was it. That was how I felt. It suppressed the crazy and the chaotic, and while it was no less sad, it had the effect of settling me. I could lean into it. I might even be able to face it because now it had a name.

Abandoned.

While you're at it, remember this truth: sadness and faith are not mutually exclusive.

If they were, you'd have to rip out vast sections of Scripture and issue apologies to key players on the biblical all-star team. Most of the middle of the Bible would be heretical. David would be canceled. Job might be asked to leave his small group. Solomon's *Vanity-of-Vanities* manuscript would be submitted for rewrites. The grief of Peter—upon-whom-I-will-build-My-church Peter—at the fireside, as the rooster crows, would be stricken from the trial transcript.

In the colorful documentary *The Jesus Music*, songwriter Bill Gaither—who sang "Something Beautiful, Something Good"—cemented that notion when he commented that most of the psalms scream to the heavens, "Where are You, God?"[3]

Not all worship songs can be up-tempo because the lives of the saints rarely are.

Let's look at an esteemed figure I don't think is talked about in this context of sadness: Mary, Jesus' mother. One needn't argue that this woman is central to the unfolding of God's story.

Mary issued one of the most beautiful and poetic passages in Scripture, bursting with the faith of an innocent.

> My soul glorifies the Lord
> and my spirit rejoices in God my Savior,
> for he has been mindful
> of the humble state of his servant.
> From now on all generations will call me blessed,
> for the Mighty One has done great things for me—
> holy is his name. (Luke 1:46–49)

Is it too outrageously irreverent to wonder if, after the initial endorphin spike of Gabriel's visit, a wistful sadness might not also have crept into the shadows in the room?

I don't think that a young Hebrew girl was unlike any other ingenue, with dreams of how her love story might unfold. I suspect she felt some misgivings knowing that she would have to forfeit hearty and heartfelt celebratory wishes and accept instead the sidelong glances and murmured whispers from childhood friends about her condition.

STAND IN YOUR PAIN

What about after Jesus' birth? Escaping Herod's horrific massacre of the innocents in Bethlehem's borders, the sudden move to Egypt— can you imagine the trauma? Only to have Simeon, a prophet, add to it with his temple pronouncement directed to Mary: "And a sword will pierce your own soul too" (Luke 2:35).

Nothing like an old-fashioned dark prophecy to usher in a little postpartum depression.

It would be akin to sending a baby present to a friend along with the note, "I'm so thrilled to welcome your little one, but you're going to experience indescribable pain as a result of his arrival." I'm sure any mother would burst into song after reading that.

You can trust God, desire His will, and be sad all at the same time. Period.

Sadness and faith often hunker down in the same space; in fact, they work in tandem to deepen our faith and translate our sadness.

> You can trust God, desire His will, and be sad all at the same time. Period.

Sadness longs to return to the familiar, even if it hurts, even if the familiar thing is irreconcilably altered or, frankly, not there anymore. Simultaneously, it feels like faith enjoys recklessly propelling you forward to the edge of a borderless abyss, like a zip line ride over a horizonless rainforest.

I recall a young woman's testimony in a Celebrate Recovery meeting where she described the trauma of her abusive childhood. Collectively, her story took our breath away. Happily, she landed with a caring foster family who wanted to adopt her. When she stood before the judge who would grant the legality of this new redeemed relationship, however, she stood terrified and transfixed.

"If I take a new last name," she wondered, "how will my real family ever find me again?"

All of us in the room let out a reflexive sigh.

Even with the promise of a brighter future, she longed to return to the familiar, as bad as it was. That testimony stayed with me a very long time. Eventually, its implications and the memory of its lesson nudged me forward with my own decisions.

It's mucky and messy and a tug o' war between your head recognizing the truth of the present reality and your heart yearning for the impossible past.

It's what one of my pastors, in spiritual terms, identified as the "now and not yet." The unresolved pain—the now—and the promise of future reconciliation of that pain—the not yet—all huddled in the same foxhole.

Just like I don't like pain, I don't like tension. We hear a lot about the kingdom of God being in this annoying now-and-not-yet juxtaposition where it's here and now, but not totally, because it's coming too. I would prefer if things were black and white—distinctly one way or the other—either totally now or totally not yet. I find myself mumbling, "Well, which is it?"

I don't think I'm alone.

How could I settle into any kind of comfort on this tightwire that relied upon two opposing forces keeping it taut and uncomfortable? Could grief spawn gratitude? Could uncertainty and mystery flourish alongside trust? Could unanswered questions, honest debate, and searching dialogue breathe the same air as an unwavering faith? Could being misunderstood strengthen your identity? Could the best be seen in the worst?

Yes, yes, and more yes.

———

I think I was pounding chicken breasts the day the thought occurred to me. The recipe for chicken piccata called for tenderizing the chicken. Who are we kidding? There was nothing tender about pulverizing that boneless breast with a spiked metal mallet. (Why would it be called tenderizing and not just called a whuppin'?)

As Jesus followers, opposites and opposite meanings surround us, yet we squirm when we have to be in their presence. I don't like that my heart becomes softer because it has been hurt. I want to develop a tender spirit without the mallet, like slowly sautéing it in butter or cream and white wine. Once again, Jesus' way is not the way that I would do it at all.

In the midst of great sorrow and searing disappointment, though, I saw my children's character skyrocket. Although they were adults at the time of my separation and divorce, it caused intense emotional and spiritual turmoil. A deep sadness moved in. Deconstructing ideas about who they believed their parents to be and accepting who they were proved traumatizing. Turns out, they were traversing the highest wire of their lives without a net, yet it grew their faith and matured them as humans exponentially. I will always remember those days with shock, yes, but with an overwhelming awe.

This is where I break the theatrical fourth wall—the invisible boundary between the actors and the audience—and speak directly to the peanut gallery: "Kids, you are remarkable human beings. Are you sure we're genetically linked? Please cancel that 23andMe test. I'm afraid to find out."

I think I have learned to exhale and relax into the "God still loves me even if I don't have all the answers" posture. I remember a pastor asking me once, after sensing my need to know every what, when, and why, "Since when did you become the Holy Spirit?"

I didn't like that. Or I should say, I didn't like that then. I came to appreciate that not only was I *not* the Holy Spirit, I didn't have to *be* the Holy Spirit, which, when it sunk in, provided great relief.

Now that I think about that example, I recognize it once more as kind of a now-and-not-yet thing. In the "now," I felt confused and angry when that "I am not the Holy Spirit" comment was shared, but later on, I saw the fullness of his insight and appreciated the bigger picture. Maybe I should write that counselor a thank-you note thirty years later.

Enlightenment: the "not yet" doesn't always travel in the fast lane.

———————

It was a Saturday night when the chimes indicated two messages. The first contained one subject that I hated: Less money; the following message held one that I loved: Congratulations.

Before clicking on either, I thought to myself, *Do we have to continue in this push-and-pull life?*

Could the salmon ever stop swimming upstream?

Could I ever catch a break and catch my breath?

The answers in order: yes, no, and maybe.

Opposing forces of tension that are integral to this now-not-yet kingdom include sorrow, uncertainty, unanswered questions, disappointments, and, at the same time, celebration, faithfulness, trustworthiness, justice. Sometimes all of these will be experienced at once.

Finally, standing in your pain recognizes that while coping mechanisms work well as temporary solutions, they were not designed to persist and settle into long-term patterns or long-term resolutions. Commit to evaluating your coping skills with a professional and asking yourself if you still need that tool, or if it's time to put it back in the shed.

I've heard this described as standing with an open umbrella long after the rain has passed. Like allowing coping skills to go stale long past their expiration date.

I might add that it's standing with an umbrella to the exclusion of being able to hold anything else in your hand. This analogy recalls images of my three-year-old grandson, Tig, refusing to take off his mossy-green alligator rain boots, even after our walk in the puddles had ended and the sidewalks were dry. Soon, though, the heat and the rub and the growing blisters of those stiff rubber wellies on a sunny day prompted him to pull them off on his own. He recognized that their usefulness had passed.

We're not supposed to be on a first-name basis with "fight or flight." Those twins were meant for small snippets in time that required an immediate response—perhaps perceived as life-threatening—to a problem that should dissipate or go away entirely. Adrenaline should not be your drug of choice, as it was mine. Staying in this fight-or-flight mode of hypervigilance needs to be offset by new processes—something we'll explore in chapter 8.

As a reminder, I am not an academic or mental health practitioner. Although I studied psychology for a short time as a grad student, my insight here has been solely gained from my own experience with traumatic loss. I'm simply sharing what worked for me, with the belief that these processes are not unique to my healing alone.

Multiple therapists and professionals, as well as a caring non-professional community, poured into my life and walked alongside me through my losses. While it would be lovely to imagine a world where professional care is available to everyone and everyone is willing and able to access it, that is never going to be true. As caring "neighbors," in the sense of Jesus' defining intent for His followers, we all can learn strategies to inform a healing path for those who cross ours.

Whatever the pathway, healing all starts with recognizing the pain and refusing to run from it. Stand in the pain. Acknowledge its discomfort, and as you begin to move through it, believe that it will produce things in you that one day will enable you to stand with someone else.

Tzatziki, Greek Chicken, and the Greek Feast

Tzatziki

Think of this as the Greeks' answer to America's ketchup.
It goes on everything.

INGREDIENTS

½ English cucumber

1 teaspoon fine sea salt, plus more to taste

1 cup high-quality Greek yogurt (you can use fat-free but full-fat will be richer)

1 to 2 tablespoons fresh lemon juice

Handful fresh dill, chopped

Sea salt to taste

DIRECTIONS

1. Slice the cucumber in half lengthwise and cut into thin slices. Or grate it using a large-holed grater. Sprinkle with 1 teaspoon of the salt and wrap in a paper towel. Let sit for 20 minutes. Squeeze out excess moisture through the paper towel.

2. Combine the squeezed cucumber, yogurt, lemon juice, and dill in a small bowl. Season to taste with the sea salt. Refrigerate until time to serve. Serve with pita bread or veggies and olives for a simple appetizer platter. Also accompanies grilled chicken nicely.

Greek Chicken with Lemon-Garlic Potatoes
To serve with Tzatziki

I serve this with Greek salad (basically tomatoes, cucumbers, olives, and feta tossed with a simple olive oil and vinegar dressing) with piles of pita bread and a small bowl of cool tzatziki. Hurling plates optional (okay, preferable).

MARINADE

1/2 cup high-quality olive oil

1 teaspoon lemon zest

4 tablespoons freshly squeezed lemon juice

1 tablespoon honey

1 tablespoon minced garlic (approximately 2 to 3 cloves)

1 teaspoon Dijon mustard

1 1/2 teaspoons salt

1/2 teaspoon ground black pepper

Leaves from 2 sprigs fresh thyme

1/4 teaspoon dried oregano

CHICKEN AND POTATOES

4 chicken breasts, boneless, skin on* (the butcher can do this for you)

1 pound baby Yukon Gold potatoes

DIRECTIONS

1. To prepare the marinade mix together the olive oil, lemon zest and juice, honey, garlic, mustard, salt, pepper, thyme, and oregano. I put the ingredients in a glass jar and shake well.

2. To prepare the chicken, place the chicken breasts in a zip-top plastic bag and add half of the marinade. Reserve the rest of the marinade for the potatoes. Refrigerate the chicken overnight or at least 2 hours.

3. To prepare the potatoes, place them in a big pot and cover with water. Bring to a boil and cook until they can be pierced easily with a knife. Do not cook until soft and falling apart. They will finish cooking in the oven. Let cool and refrigerate until ready to roast.

4. When you're ready to cook the meal, remove the potatoes and chicken breasts from the refrigerator and let them sit on the counter for 30 minutes to bring them to room temperature.

5. Preheat the oven to 425 degrees.

6. Place the chicken on a foil-covered baking sheet, skin-side up. Place the potatoes in a bowl and toss with the remaining marinade. Place the potatoes on the same baking sheet, if room allows, or on their own foil-covered sheet if it's too crowded.

7. Roast for 35 minutes. The skin on the chicken should be golden brown. After removing from the oven, lightly tent the baking sheet(s) with foil and let the chicken rest for 15 to 20 minutes.

8. After the meat rests, cut across the breast in thin slices. Plate next to the lemon-garlic potatoes and a crisp Greek salad.

Makes 4 servings.

*Cook's note: Roasting a chicken breast with the skin on gives it a deep golden-brown color that is so much more appetizing to serve.

CHAPTER 5

FIND SOME FRIENDS
WITH STRETCHERS

Some people care too much. I think it's called love.
—WINNIE THE POOH (A. A. MILNE)

CAN WE TALK?

Is it just me, or do you, too, think we often gloss over that story about the friends cutting the hole in the roof to land their paralyzed pal at the feet of Jesus?

Let me remind you of how that story goes.

A few days later, when Jesus again entered Capernaum, the people heard that he had come home. They gathered in such large numbers that there was no room left, not even outside the door, and he preached the word to them. Some men came, bringing to him a paralyzed man, carried by four of them. Since they could not get him to Jesus because of the crowd, they made an opening in the roof above Jesus by digging through it and then lowered the mat the man was lying on. When Jesus saw their faith, he said to the paralyzed man, "Son, your sins are forgiven." (Mark 2:1–5)

I could, perhaps, credit that gloss-over to hearing it told in Sunday school an infinite number of times, accompanied each time by a colorful flannelgraph, which might tend to oversimplify the story.

Who doesn't love bright, felty cutouts covering the board with soft, pliable, primary-colored shapes, casting such simplicity onto a story that would normally have us pestering the teller with hard-hitting investigative questions like, "What? They did *what*? To whom? And they put him *where*?"

I've remodeled several houses. I've witnessed the messiness—and the fun—of demolition. Trust me, you don't want to be standing underneath a sledgehammer and its aftermath.

I'd be stopping Luke in his recitation and protesting.

"Wait, wait, wait!"

Slow down, Doc.

"They cut a hole in the roof? With what? And put him in front of who?"

Isn't that narrative just a little bit weird? I understand that I'm visualizing this with a twenty-first-century, Western context, and an imagination shaped by television shows of home renovation before-and-afters.

I mean, winding it back twenty centuries, maybe people were sawing sunroofs in houses all over town. No space at the poker table Monday night? No problem. I'll just bring my Craftsman power saw along.

Scripture indicates it was all men holding the stretcher, but let me tell you about my mom. She rearranged the furniture every day when we kids were at school, sliding couches and tables and beds from one room to the next to quench some pre-HGTV home-improvement obsession. One day, though, mere rearranging failed to satisfy. Stumbling across an ax (not sure how one "stumbles" upon an ax), she decided to hack out a wall. Took it right down to the studs.

When my dad got home from work, she greeted him at the door with, "Mel, we'll be remodeling now."

She could've been in that rooftop demo crew, hands down. Probably could've dug it out single-handedly. But I digress.

Allow me to digress a bit more.

An overwhelmingly impressive lesson I learned during my Holy Land travels was how impossible it is for the Western world to grasp the Eastern one. Honestly, we are nothing alike, and I'm not sure if before that trip I ever cared to sort through the differences.

Take the variety of people groups—the bedouins, for instance. Wanderers. I had envisioned Omar Sharif look-alikes—google *Dr. Zhivago*, kids—with flowing linen caftans and headscarves, majestically herding their sheep across the desert. Instead, I witnessed poor shepherds, Middle Eastern gypsies, more like outcasts, misunderstood by others outside their tribe. Our guide told us that a government agency had allotted funds to build structures that they might sleep inside with a roof overhead. Instead, as was their preference, they herded the *animals* inside and laid their bedrolls back under the stars. I wondered if these desert nomads were less like Lawrence of Arabia and more like the version of the shepherds in Bethlehem's fields.

I couldn't picture the little drummer boy anywhere among them.

Take sociology, and add in a little topography.

Israel is basically rock with sand scattered on top. There aren't thick forests shooting deep roots into moist, loamy soil from which fresh-sawn lumber flows. The houses stood with stone walls, and perhaps Jesus was adept as a cutter of those stones, as opposed to a carpenter skilled solely with wood. And that manger? Might it have been more like a cave than the rustic A-frame crèche on the front lawn of the Little Lighthouse Church in my neighborhood—the one we admire from the maple-bacon donut shop across the street?

Then there's resources.

Water is scarce and prized and fought over. When Jesus went to a well, He knew other people would show up too. It wasn't an option. Dry throats from dry climates initiated so many opening inquiries into searching conversations. Thirst, spiritual and otherwise, persisted as a daily reality. As a result, when Jesus talked about living water, they would have sat up and listened.

Some of these facts remain just interesting cultural footnotes, not making much difference in how we perceive Jesus' messages. But others color our comprehension and strengthen an account's clarity. Tweak a tale's intent.

Let's revisit the narrative of the paralytic on the stretcher. "The people heard that he [Jesus] had come home" (v. 1).

"Home," likely a typical Galilean house, constructed with sides of roughly hewn blocks of stone. Obviously, stone wouldn't go onto the roof, so what was lying around in great supply? Palm fronds. The weather was mild, very little rain, so why not? The roof probably consisted of a few wooden beams, perhaps flexible branches, covered with layers of broad leaves and smooth mud, the consistency of clay soil, which most gardeners detest but most participants in reality TV shows, like *Survivor*, prize for its ability to "plaster" spaces between fronds and beams.

That dirt between palm fronds isn't the same as a two-story, French-inspired farmhouse with heavy, oak-beamed ceilings. Why, with that European architecture, we can hardly imagine climbing on top of the roof to hang our Christmas lights, or to affix that old-school Santa sleigh and reindeer thing, let alone chop a hole in it with the neighborhood wrecking crew.

Conversely, the East-enders of the narrative could easily imagine pulling back the palms, punching out the dried dirt of the rooftop with some sharp rocks or shards of broken tiles, and in their vigor, kicking in a willowy branch or two. None of which would send those below to urgent care.

Heck, my mom could've done it without an ax.

I also know that all of this is not the point. I realize the point is that Jesus is doing something highly inflammatory by healing this man in the manner that He did. Teasing out the implications for the bystanders with all that talk about forgiving sins and daring to overlay the act of healing with the act of spiritual cleansing. More insulting to the Pharisees present than the healing itself was Jesus announcing Himself as the "One who can swipe away the sins."

Also known as *God*.

There is a secondary point, though, that isn't lost on people like me, who are so, so grateful for the friends in my life. The point is this: we need friends with stretchers when we're broken.

> We need friends with stretchers when we're broken.

Not only that. I have to ask myself, Would I be—am I—the kind of friend who finds herself desperate to help my broken friends get well? Would I be scouting out the rooftop and reassuring the man on the mat that this encounter was a done deal? Or would I be catching my breath and suggesting that we just come back another day when the parking lot wasn't so full?

After one of our regular Sunday dinners, I remember my twenty-something oldest son arranging the chairs in the living room and gesturing in a way that meant, "Mom, sit there." It looked strangely like an intervention scene from a doctor-show drama I had just watched on Hulu.

Hmm. Something's up.

I appreciated the words that followed, as hard as they fell. The content of that message really doesn't matter in this writing. What does stand out in my memory, though, remains the message's pointed postscript.

"Mom, you have so many people who love you. Yet you sit in this brokenness with those who do not."

The next day I filed for divorce.

I might as well have been the man on the mat.

Those kids and their spouses cut a hole in my roof and lowered me to the feet of Jesus that night.

Name someone who wants you to get well, because to stand in your pain, you need others who will stand with you. Go ahead, write down their names. Satan will always nudge us to isolation, not engagement. We may not believe that we are worth it, but someone else does.

I wasn't worth getting well for.

My reliably negative ruminations reminded me of that. My kids were worth it, though, so like me, if you can't see or sense or believe in your own value, weigh the hope, pleas, and prayers of those who care about you.

Sometimes we will do for others what we will not do for ourselves.

I sucked my breath in and stacked the scales with dreams my kids held for my future as a grandmother, knowing that this role was irreplaceable in the positive impact I could have on those littles. I meticulously measured the times of encouragement that I could provide for my adult children as they would face challenges yet to be announced. I carefully counted out the prayers and petitions that I could offer to other "unexpected widows" like me, who didn't have the support systems I did. I could almost smell the chicken soup I could simmer for the sick and the celebrating alike. When I did these things, the scales tipped decidedly in one direction.

I was worth it.

You are worth it.

What kind of a future do others envision for you when you just can't see past your morning bowl of overnight oats?

Be aware, however. Shame battles that metric, doggedly trying to weigh down the scale on the opposite side to offset your emotional gains. Shame was the source of those mental ruminations that echoed my worthlessness. Shame seamlessly scripted negative internal dialogue and kept me hypervigilant as I evaluated people and situations that might make me feel vulnerable and unsafe.

Some people would ask why I felt shame for all that I had been through. That intrigued me, too, as at first it didn't make much sense. While I certainly was far from perfect, faithfulness and fidelity were central to my character. My vows were kept as precious to me, and I couldn't control the catastrophic loss of income or the cardiac complications that cropped up and threatened to alter my life. I wasn't even home when my house caught on fire, and Lord knows, I wasn't the one on my phone when the teenager behind me failed to stop on the 405 when the traffic slowed.

Logically, there was no reason for me to own any shame. I had endured repeated losses and was navigating them the best way I could in the company of caring people. It would have been appropriate to feel proud of the courage it took to evaluate and process these intense changes.

I couldn't deny shame's existence though.

As someone who forever tried to do my very best with whatever I put my hand to, I felt embarrassed that I had not been able to snap out of it.

In my mind, again, emotion always trumped logic.

Wasn't I stronger than this?

Am I really that weak and pathetic?

The shame was suffocating.

You may sense the weight of shame too. It's sneaky, how it fails to stick to Teflon-coated perpetrators but finds such a fertile home in the hurts of those wounded by them. Social constructs of "pulling yourself up by your bootstraps" only intensify our shame and make us want to hide our problems more. There is a reason that shaming—I think of it as the bullying we do to ourselves—proves so potent. It's effective 100 percent of the time. Its efficacy? Legendary.

We women pull out our handy-dandy tape measure, kept conveniently so close at hand.

"I can measure that shortcoming of mine. Absolutely. Of course, I already know the answer, but I'm happy to oblige. I love reminding myself of my inadequacies."

Then we painstakingly lay down that ruler next to some imagined saint—hint, they don't exist, so stop looking—who we've mistakenly crowned Princess Perfect. We routinely come up short. Even if the comparison is subconscious, it remains a powerful reminder of our souls' scarcity after traumatic events suck us dry.

Author and "Budgetnista" Tiffany Aliche, dealing with her audience's financial failings, said it so well: "It's difficult to shed shame on your own. Friends help you to normalize the process of resolving that shame or grief or mistakes."[1]

Friends with stretchers—or a deep mug of coffee and a listening ear, scones help too—facilitate shame's shedding, dragging it out of the darkness into the light, deconstructing its false narratives while reinforcing the strength you need to tackle it.

———

Standing in the aisle of the big-box store, staring at the Baby Yoda LEGO set, I snapped a photo to send to my daughter-in-law along with the following message:

> The box says age 10. Can the boys handle this? There's a
> zillion pieces.

Attach photo.

Add crazy, googly-eyed emoji (me).

Send.

Incoming FaceTime call. From the Wonder Boys who now regularly answer their mom's phone.

Two thumbs-up light up my screen. "Yeah, Nana. We got this. Why would you think we couldn't do this?"

Sheesh. The kid's seven.

When I admire the intricate designs those twins can build, I only see two things. Time and tiny pieces—my aching bare feet can attest to LEGO's myriad and sharp-edged shapes. So many little tiles interlocking one upon another. An endless mountain of parts, a 3D plastic puzzle imagined by some Rubik's Cube–raised, genius child prodigy somewhere, obviously.

Ugh. I'd lose my mind if I had to assemble this thing. Hence, crazy, googly-eyed emoji from me. I'd pull out all my eyebrows before I'd unpack that nightmare.

That's how shame builds—one tiny brick at a time and never all at once—like the Baby Yoda LEGO set that sent chills down my spine. That's also, though, how shame finds its demise. With you and your neighborhood wrecking crew dismantling one tile at a time, never all at once. Together.

"Lowering a friend to the feet of Jesus" looks like a lot of different things. The Baby Yoda demo people for sure. But there are others.

I'm going to share several things people did that helped me. They may also help you, if not to lessen your own load, perhaps to lessen a load for a friend, who at this very moment may be waiting on a mat for a hooligan with a handsaw.

These points may be useful to articulate what "help" looks like to you. They may shake some ideas from your tree, so that you can find a voice for your needs. Mostly, I think this process serves to inform those around you as to what may be some intentional real-time ways to help those who are facing an acute loss. It's not a list cast in con-crete. Brainstorm with others, using this as a starting point.

Also note that many of the people who helped me were not my age. Not my contemporaries or peers. They were much younger, which was interesting to experience. The role reversal of younger helping elder took me a while to fully embrace, but I grew to appre-ciate that it was filling their cups too.

Some things that young people did to help me in very inten-tional ways:

- My son's small group showed up one Saturday morning with donuts and coffee and cleaned and organized my garage. It actually made a dreaded task fun. Okay, well, maybe that's a stretch, but it wasn't awful.
- Some other young women helped me prepare and run several garage sales, as money—even a little bit—was so helpful. It felt rewarding and empowering, when so much did not. More importantly, when clutter left, some of the chaos left too. It was hard to see so many sad souvenirs of a former life get disman-tled, and they understood. When the tandem bike was hauled away, no one had to say anything because their hugs said it all.
- Other young people helped me with questions I had about my computer. And they didn't start the instruction with, "Oh, it's so easy." They knew none of the simplest things were easy for me then. It was more like, "It feels hard, doesn't it? But we can help you fix that."
- My daughter's best friend would invite me to coffee and insist we have whipped cream on top. Sometimes I just sat there and stared. That was just fine with her. Then we drained the last drop and headed home. I'm sure she thought nothing was happening with this woman (me), yet each time we met

I appreciated the whipped cream more, and I started to smile when I saw the barista mound it in my cup.

- My daughter went through my closet and lined up outfits for me to wear to job interviews or just to get out of the house—and out of my bathrobe. She went through the bills and in bright red ink marked on a new wall calendar when things needed to be paid.

- Afterward, I would discover a herd of pink Post-its on my bathroom mirror with new messaging for me to read. "You are beautiful. You can get through today, Mom. Love you."

- When I needed to move, young women showed up to help me pack and box up donated items. They made it possible to give away those extraneous things I didn't need to drag into a new life. Before Marie Kondo, they reminded me where to find joy and where *not* to find it. Clearly, not with five juicers and three blenders.

- For a period of time I was without a car after mine was totaled in a freeway collision. A college student, who was visiting his girlfriend for a couple of weeks, just tossed his keys to me and said, "Hey. Take mine."

- Others made room for me at church. When they saw me come in, they flagged me down and gave me a seat, which made me feel less alone and so included. They sought me out at coffee time afterward and initiated conversation that made me feel seen. It's so easy to avoid a "sad old lady," but they made a beeline for me nonetheless.

- Some helped me with car repairs or meals or just stopped by the house to check in on me and say hi for ten minutes. Some of the "kids" had such a gift for fun and laughter, and their presence always lifted the darkness.

- Many prayed for me and over me. More of those stories ahead.

Two particularly touching gestures will stay with me forever.

"First" holidays after a loss mark dreaded days on the calendar. Following the death of a spouse, discovery of an affair, or a separation or divorce, Valentine's Day ranks among the worst. My first February 14 found me crying again, except this time, happy tears flowed.

Waiting on the front porch for me sat a pretty pink bouquet with the following tag attached: "I love you more than the heavens and the earth. I will never leave you nor forsake you. I will be with you always! Happy Valentine's Day! Love, God"

To this day, I have no idea who sent the flowers.

I mean, other than God.

I saved that note, and every year when December 31 comes, I move it from the calendar's last February home and reattach it to the new calendar's pages. My New Year's tasks are not complete until those words fill up the blank square on February 14.

How thoughtful. How kind. How inventive. How unforgettable this anonymous gift of love.

Second, I'll never forget day one of our Sarah's hospice care and the cacophony of decisions and heartbreaking conversations. The hospital bed was ordered and set up in the living room, and then the delivery men turned and waved goodbye.

My son KC and I stopped them and asked, "Can you help us lift our friend onto the bed?

"No, we don't do that, ma'am."

Really? These are the things that no one tells you. Of course, you don't ask because you don't even know what to ask. Sarah's face flushed red with embarrassment. It made her feel like a nuisance.

KC picked up his phone and walked outside. Ten minutes later, three cars raced up to the front of the house and three of his friends ran up to the porch. Together, they lovingly lifted Sarah, who was a big woman, onto her bed. It took strength, for sure. KC and I couldn't have done it on our own. More than strength, they offered her dignity, did it with humility, and showered her with discretion and respect.

Four men. With a friend. On a stretcher of sorts.

I suspect there's a tendency for some young people to think there's nothing they could do for someone their parents' age—that they are ill-equipped or not experienced enough, but trust me, "love your neighbor" has never felt so real to me. Small church groups can particularly make an impact here, though God will also lead individuals to do things in a quiet way for people in grief. It's exciting to pray for God to lead you to a hurting heart and then to wait. Expectantly. It's like you're a spiritual undercover agent.

> It's exciting to pray for God to lead you to a hurting heart and then to wait.

When grief makes a splash, some people you know will run for cover and some will grab their raincoats and run your way. Some friends will be unable to enter into your pain. Period. I don't know how to say it any other way. If the brokenness makes them uneasy, they won't be present. You will find that out automatically. You won't have to ask.

MY STRETCHER PEOPLE WITH CREATIVE WAYS TO HELP

The ones with the raincoats running in my direction? Those were my stretcher people, and the way they cared proved life-altering for my family and me. Their resources and intelligence, creativity, humor, selflessness, generosity, and kindness knew no bounds. They shone in the darkness and gave me so much to celebrate.

See if this list doesn't inspire you to be a stretcher person for someone else:

- During my deepest grieving, my three children all became engaged and were married. Glorious timing—ugh. These days were nothing like I had envisioned they would be. *My friends painted new visions though.* All their engagement parties, showers, and weddings were collaborations of people who showed up offering houses to host, meals to make, design ideas to test, flowers to fashion. My college friends traveled out of state to help with my oldest's reception decor and to keep me smiling. The morning of my daughter's March outdoor wedding, an army of mom-and-daughter teams set the dinner tables, folded the napkins, and then covered them all with plastic while the showers passed. Likewise, with my youngest son's wedding, the volunteers outnumbered the fears I held, including the couple who said, "Hey, have the wedding here. It will be great in our backyard."

- Knowledgeable and resourceful businesspeople volunteered to advise me on finances, debt, insurance, and tax problems. None of this was easy. It was humiliating, but none of them ever treated me any differently than if I were their best client.

- Emotional care knew no bounds. Countless coffees, conversations, conferences. Together we wrote responses to questions I might get from people on the street, to help me feel less tongue-tied. They drove me to medical appointments and outpatient surgeries to free up my kids so they could work. They were always available to be a second set of ears to help me understand a medical procedure or a therapy or a problem.

- Dear friends sent me Bible verses daily, which I printed and taped up to my "wailing wall." I read them every morning. When I moved, a forward-thinking friend took them down for me and tucked them into a notebook, my own personal book of Psalms—one small step to moving past the lament.

Encouraging cards I got in the mail were stuck in my Bible and in the stacks of books I was reading. I still have many of them. Cherished bookmarks.

- A couple from my small group had an extra car they loaned me for a couple of months following my accident. I barely knew them.
- Another couple would regularly come by and help me with handyman-type tasks like hanging pictures or curtain rods.
- My friends looked for odd jobs that I could do with my new medical limitations. Organizing a kitchen. Dog-sitting. House-sitting. Some light catering and housecleaning. Event planning. Odd writing jobs. I could only rise to the level I felt capable of, and shame was shedding slowly. *Write a book? Are you kidding me? I don't even know my name.*
- I couldn't count the meals my older sister and her husband cooked for me. The bed in their guest room became a second home. Conversation lingered late into the night. All without chiding me for the speed of my healing—ranked up there with the velocity of tar flowing down a sloping street in the middle of winter.
- My younger sister showed up with Thai food, a really great used car, and lots of laughter and promises of "One day you will look outside and see the branches blooming, and say, 'Oh, what do you know? The branches are blooming.' Now, have you tried that coconut soup?"
- My brother-in-law, a busy attorney, took time to help me with a nasty small-claims case in which I was the defendant and translated legalese for me during my divorce. He sat with me in court, along with my sons.
- My dearest and longest friends opened up their guest bedroom every Wednesday night for *years*, folding me into their Bible study, feeding me, and doing their brand of talk therapy at the

kitchen table. As I type this, I sit at a desk in their dream retirement home, where they opened the door for two weeks and said, "Come. Write here."

- One friend regularly took castoffs to Goodwill for me and helped me clean out Sarah's closet when I was ready. My friend's husband posted things on eBay for me, helping me sell old china or collectibles, once prized but now no longer important to me. The online selling sites felt complicated and daunting, and it was nice to have a man who would interact with the buyers I did not know. As a professional videographer, he made videos for me and my kids for all the special occasions, something we couldn't afford otherwise.

- Some friends were movie friends and some friends were praying friends and some friends were walking friends and some were "talk in the booth for hours" friends. To this day, I laugh thinking about the restaurant my pal Virginia and I closed down and then walked out of without paying because our conversation was so intense. Don't worry. They got their money, but when it hit us, we laughed until our stomachs ached. Clearly I was on the road to perdition.

- "McDonald's Therapy Sessions" (easier to scrape up coffee money for that) became stand-up comedy sessions with a crazy Swedish friend of mine. We laughed until we cried. Mostly at ourselves. It wasn't always a conversation about problems. It was chatting about the episodes in life that we found amusing, and our lives so readily supplied the scripting. Some of you are really good at making people laugh. Use that gift.

- My college friends met with me monthly to review my plans and my progress, to hear about my heartbreak and my headaches. Those ladies can cook, and they took good stabs at fattening me up. Patience doesn't even begin to describe their care for me.

"Stretcher people" remind you of all the things they know you can do well, and the strengths they know you possess. It doesn't matter to them that you're Jell-O. That's just today. Tomorrow, they know you can be better. They never stop telling you so.

———————

LEGO bricks galore tumbled onto the table. Before I knew it, I imagined brightly colored bricks of my dismantled grief all over the place. Small. Tiny, in fact. Indistinguishable as anything at all.

This is what Jesus meant when He said, "Love your neighbor as yourself." It's real, gritty, unglamorous, annoying, frustrating, inconvenient, costly, time intensive, and repetitive. Basically, a pain in the neck. Did I mention annoying?

And it's exactly what love looks like.

For me, Jesus' words have held the greatest promise in the Bible. And Jesus' last words have embedded themselves deeply within my heart. Looking at John and His mother standing by John's side, what did He say with the waning breath that gave each exquisite word rarity and weight?

> When Jesus saw his mother there, and the disciple whom he loved standing nearby, he said to her, "Woman, here is your son," and to the disciple, "Here is your mother." From that time on, this disciple took her into his home. (John 19:26–27)

The last moments of His intense suffering held equally intense concern and compassion for Mary. In this ancient culture, Jesus knew her life without a husband and her oldest son would be dismally compromised.

Sometimes I wonder if underneath modern sociological changes, we've really made as much progress as we think. Women have come a long way, for sure—after all, I am a child of the sixties, which is a book for another day—but an older, single woman remains just about the least valued of all demographics, even today. Trust me. I felt it.

For some women, add to it racial discrimination and economic distress and entrenched social structures, and they don't have a chance.

Jesus knew all these things. He was saying more than for *one disciple* to care for *one woman*. I believe it was a call to the church to care for the widows and all who could be labeled as marginalized. It can start with small bullet points showing one widow in one church community or neighborhood that she is not alone.

A new family picture was painted that day at the foot of the cross, with the church becoming the family and Jesus' words echoing to the now and not yet, today's generation and those to come. We, the church—framed by the excruciating final exchange between Jesus and His disciple—can do much to make a difference.

If we spent as much time helping people in the margins as we do arguing over our differences, what could happen?

Wonder about that.

What do you think is said in dying words? The most relevant, most pivotal, most visceral thoughts and wishes. Very little theological debate or political posturing wet the lips of a dying soul.

"Too simplistic," one might say, to which I would wholeheartedly agree. Jesus' message is simple. It's just borderline impossible for us humans to do. Or maybe I should say, for us humans to *want* to do.

Can we concentrate on Jesus' words? Personal pain has left me with very little patience for the pedantic, ineffectual, and irrelevant discourse that fills our screens. The beauty of longer years is that they have graced me with less stridency about my need to be right—or my opinion to be heard, my way to be the "right" way. The marginalized, like Jesus' mother, get swept aside by our egos and we lose the message of these final words.

I don't want to do that. That is a wiry but strong spoke of the "my pain will not be wasted" wheel. If I learned to be more compassionate because of my pain, that is its reward.

Now it's your turn, sista.

Demonstrate a desire to be well and show measurable gains to others who are helping you.

Consider the paralytic at the pool of Bethesda in John's gospel. The one who had languished there for thirty-eight years. "When Jesus saw him lying there and learned that he had been in this condition for a long time, he asked him, 'Do you want to get well?'" (John 5:6).

Well, do you?

It's okay to answer "I don't know" or "Maybe" or, like the man in the pool did at first, "I can't, sir" (John 5:7 NLT).

It's important to show progress to those near you who are in anguish over your pain that they cannot extinguish, and in doing so, plant the seed for you to choose wellness with them. Eventually, you'll choose on your own, but in the beginning, find your friend with the stretcher and hop on.

———————

Measurable gains make the healing process seem attainable. Make a list of things that, in your mind, will show progress, and label them "hard" or "easy."

If you're analytical and live to create another Excel doc, design a chart. If you're spontaneous and don't care if you ever see a spreadsheet again, put your ideas in a hat and randomly pull out one each day—or each week.

Pick one hard thing.

- Call for a therapy appointment.
- Meet with the attorney.

- Ask my friend to go with me to my doctor's appointment.
- Call and ask my small group leader if she'll come to the court appearance with me.
- Eat three meals today.

Then one easy thing.

- Take a walk.
- Take a long walk.
- Take a longer walk.
- Wash my hair.
- Wash my clothes.
- Find my lipstick.

I always feel braver when I'm with somebody. Whether it's travel or signing your name on a karaoke list, it's nice to have a friend along.

And on the other side, it is so good to enter into someone else's pain and *to stay.*

There is relational reward in that, and all those humans who helped me know that now too. You may not be perfect at it, you might be afraid of it, but if you're willing, it will satisfy like nothing else can.

That's how He made us.

Chicken Soup

This is a quick version using a store-bought roasted chicken, and not one person will know or care that the chicken wasn't roasted in your kitchen. This soup seems to be a universal remedy for feeling low, and it's a lovely gift for a friend who's hurting. It looks so pretty if you deliver it in a large mason jar along with some bakery-bought rolls.

INGREDIENTS

1 store-bought roast chicken (economical and tasty)

2 tablespoons olive oil

1 onion, diced (I always use sweet onions)*

3 ribs celery, diced (I include some leafy ends, which look pretty)*

3 carrots, cut into ¼-inch "coins"*

2 to 3 sprigs fresh thyme

2 (32-ounce) cartons chicken stock

Salt, to taste

1 small bunch fresh parsley, cut or torn into small pieces

DIRECTIONS

1. Add the olive oil to a deep soup pot and heat over medium heat until simmering. Add the onions, celery, carrots, and thyme. Cook, stirring often, over medium-low heat until translucent, about 5 to 6 minutes.

2. Remove the white meat from the chicken (breasts and thighs), shredding into small pieces and reserving the rest for sandwiches and stock. (Kids love the drumsticks.) I do this with my hands, and

it falls apart into nice pieces. Add the white meat and the chicken stock to the pot.

3. Bring the soup to a boil over medium-high heat, reduce the heat to low, and simmer for 20 minutes. Add salt to taste. Because the salt content varies between stocks and roast chickens, no salt amount is indicated. You just have to taste it.

4. Garnish the individual bowls of soup with parsley right before serving. Makes 8 servings.

Cook's note: Some grocery stores offer onion, celery, and carrots already diced (called mirepoix) in their refrigerated vegetable section. Okay to substitute 1 carton.

CHAPTER 6

WHO YOU SAY I AM

With a name like Carole Holiday, I can't give
you a speeding ticket on Christmas Eve.
—HIGHWAY PATROL OFFICER, SPOKEN AS HE HELD THE DRIVER'S
LICENSE UP TO THE LIGHT THAT DECEMBER NIGHT, TO A HARRIED—
AND HURRIED—AND GUILTY-AS-CHARGED CAROLE HOLIDAY

"And you shall call His name JESUS." (Matthew 1:21 NKJV)
"And you are to call him John." (Luke 1:13)
"You will call his name Ishmael." (Genesis 16:11 NKJV)
"You shall name him Isaac." (Genesis 17:19 NASB)
"His name shall be Solomon." (1 Chronicles 22:9 KJV)
"Behold, a child, Josiah by name, shall be born to the house of
    David." (1 Kings 13:2 NKJV)

I TRY TO PUT MYSELF INTO THE SANDALS OF THOSE HEARING
these pronouncements firing directly from the mouths of angels.
Scary. Surreal. Sensational. And clearly not a time when you would

argue about the choice of names. If a glowing being hovers above me and tells me to call the kid Dancer or Prancer, Cupid or Vixen, I'm all in. The luggage is getting monogrammed.

Names matter.

They're neither random nor mundane. They stick. They label. They distinguish. They foretell, explain, elucidate, introduce. Herald. As in "Hark the Herald Angels Sing," which every English-speaking five-year-old on the planet thinks is an angel named Harold who just likes to sing.

I'm not the only one with a story about a name.

Every family has stories about names.

You could most definitely tell tales if any of your great-great-great family members immigrated to America in the years between 1892 and 1924, arriving via Ellis Island. If you did sail through New York Harbor past Lady Liberty and your last name had more than two syllables, chances are the steamer ship's manifest logged it as something more Anglicized—Kohnovalsky to Cohn, for example.

The name change, most likely done by the immigrants themselves, or perhaps by a recorder who phonetically spelled it as an American would pronounce it, held huge cultural implications. They knew that stamping a surname that marked them as foreign could set them apart, not necessarily in a good way. Their newly edited names became the visa to help them fit in, granting them access to a new and better life.

My grandmother, born Hilma, voluntarily changed her name to Thelma, not because it shed its Swedish flavor or sound but because she thought it more modern. I'm not sure what social register she consulted when thinking Thelma propelled her into the 1920s with style and sophistication and modernity.

Whatever.

If it worked for Thelma, it probably worked.

I wore a very typical name of the 1950s and 60s, but my mother distinguished my name by ending it, uncharacteristically, with the letter *e*. Later, she told me she named me after Carole Lombard, a comedic actress and blonde bombshell. She was married to the dashing Clark Gable, I hasten to add. Even though I hardly believed that was true, I slurped that story right up, thinking it lent me a bit of a starry past—if only in my mind. Kinda like Thelma.

Names are a big deal. They're like the wrapping paper with which identities are packaged.

Names are a big deal in the Bible too. Scripture strongly suggests that names matter.

Starting with Adam: "ground," as in "from the dust of the ground." And Eve, as in "mother of all the living" (Genesis 3:20). No two names draw a line between humanity and creation more directly than Adam and Eve.

Thinking back, there were twins living in my dorm at UCLA, and one was named Eve. Not a common name then or now. It fit her perfectly. A ballet dancer who glided across campus—not plodded or trotted or jogged like the rest of us ordinary humans, but glided—as if being carried along by a wave of foam. Eve had thick, cascading hair and round, doelike eyes. A twentieth-century Eve residing in my very own Rieber Hall. Imagine that.

Names in the Bible can be hard to spell.

I once was given the task of identifying the name of the oldest person in the Bible—on a game show, no less. *Methuselah*. Try doing that under the bright lights of a soundstage with the intense countenance of the handsome show host drilling you, and the hyped-up studio audience counting down the seconds, reminiscent of jeering ancient audiences in Rome's Colosseum. Methuselah is a tongue twister of a name and had me wishing I had earned more Jet Cadet badges in Old Testament memorization. Throw in Jehoshaphat, and you've got a mouthful.

Even biblical nicknames hold significance.

Like James and John being tagged with Sons of Thunder. That's a cool nickname though. A designation bestowed by Jesus that could've been borrowed by a duo of superheroes. Much better than Doubting Thomas. And certainly no one would want to be shackled with the nickname Judas, which embodies *traitor* so clearly that no other adjective need apply. One word, the proper noun, says it all.

As mentioned, select names were bestowed by angels before certain babies were born. "You shall call Him _____" reliably reigns as the centerpiece of the angel's script in every Christmas pageant. If the second-grade angel forgets her lines, it's always safe just to blurt that one out, with a few hallelujahs thrown in for good measure.

Not only was Jesus' name prescribed, but John the Baptist's as well. John and Jesus were both given their names by God Himself via the angel Gabriel. When Gabriel comes knocking, you open the door. The lofty stature of this messenger signals the message's import.

Unfortunately, Zechariah, John's dumbstruck father—literally—didn't receive the news well at first, doubting the angel's words or perhaps his own sanity (Luke 1:5–22). Can you blame him? He was leveled mute with this unlikely announcement.

Turns out, Gabriel has a short fuse.

Thankfully, for Priest Z, big things happened on the eighth day postpartum, the traditional and reverently held Hebrew day for circumcision and naming.

> On the eighth day they came to circumcise the child, and they were going to name him after his father Zechariah, but his mother spoke up and said, "No! He is to be called John." They said to her, "There is no one among your relatives who has that name." (Luke 1:59–61)

Props to Elizabeth for holding her ground. I'm sure there were murmurs.

"Woman, what are you thinking?"

Followed by the whispered, "Ask Zechariah. We know that the man will do the right thing."

Then the crowd deserted Elizabeth and cornered Zechariah for a game of charades.

> Then they made signs to his father, to find out what he would like to name the child. He asked for a writing tablet, and to everyone's astonishment he wrote, "His name is John." Immediately his mouth was opened and his tongue set free, and he began to speak, praising God." (vv. 62–64)

Game point to Elizabeth.

When Zechariah's tongue was loosed, I don't think there were too many doubters left standing to question the boy's name. Clearly, this name—John—held promise and power.

> All the neighbors were filled with awe, and throughout the hill country of Judea people were talking about all these things. Everyone who heard this wondered about it, asking, "What then is this child going to be?" For the Lord's hand was with him. (vv. 65–66)

For Jews in Jesus' time, names held particular significance. Still to this day, observant Jews celebrate a bris (the Jewish rite of circumcision) when the baby turns eight days old. Males are circumcised by the rabbi and the name made official. Usually the child's name shares at least a letter with an important relative, establishing a bond with the family of origin.

Recall the objections voiced to John's mother about his name not being connected to a family member: "There is no one among your relatives who has that name" (v. 61).

My friends Mike and Karen named their son Matthew, to share the same first letter with his dad, Michael, but also to honor both grandfathers, Morris and Menachem, and a brother, Maury. M&M'S everywhere, because names firmly fix family connections.

Those in my generation witnessed the embedded attachment of a name to one's roots in cinematic detail in the blockbuster television miniseries, Alex Haley's *Roots*. It provided an unforgettable look at the significance of what we choose to call our children. Set in the dark genesis of the New World's slave trade, it centers around a defiant and proud Gambian man who never forgets his true family's name, despite attempts to make him answer to his false name, Toby.

The most iconic scene in the series, and one viewers could recount beat by beat, remains undisputed. With strong arms lifting his ebony infant to the sky, the African father proclaims, "You are Kunta Kinte, son of Omoro Kinte—your name is your spirit. Your name is your shield."[1]

I can't tell you how many of our friends stood in newborn nurseries holding their newborn high, recreating this scene for proud grandparents' cameras. Today, it would have been a TikTok moment for sure.

When I was about seven, the Jewish family next door hosted a bris ceremony for Baby Ronald. With a clear view of the festivities, I sat at my bedroom window rapt with wonder, as a big-bearded man with a big black hat and a big black bag strolled up their driveway. I heard that he gave the baby a thimbleful of wine. When I asked my mom and dad (true teetotalers) why he would do that, they told me they would explain it in a few years. I'm still waiting.

Somehow, though, despite the cryptic messaging, I sensed the importance of giving this baby a name. Strangely and sadly, when he died suddenly a few months later, I felt comforted by the fact that such a big deal had been made of his life when he was just a bit older than one week. It made me feel like no one would ever forget him. Even as a child, I remained fascinated by this celebration over a name and sensed it was an event our Jewish friends held sacred for good reason.

———

Names could be changed in the Bible. So while God could grant names, it was also true that He could erase and then replace them.

In really epic scenarios, God renamed people. Picked a whole new name for them.

Abram became Abraham. Sarai became Sarah. Jacob became Israel. In each of those cases, the secondary name was a much-improved moniker. These new names, in particular, held blessings for a future bright with unexpected favor.

God has promised that someday He will give us a new name too.

> *I will give you a good name*, a name of distinction,
> among all the nations of the earth,
> as I restore your fortunes before their very eyes.
> I, the LORD, have spoken!
>
> (ZEPHANIAH 3:20 NLT, EMPHASIS ADDED)

Are you getting the idea that names are a big deal to God?

They're significant, chockablock with meaning. Threading neat running stitches between our past, present, and future.

I figure if God bothers with this sort of ordinary business of naming, it's probably not so ordinary after all.

So what is it with names? What prompted Solomon, the wealthiest man alive, to write, "A good name is more desirable than great riches; to be esteemed is better than silver or gold" (Proverbs 22:1)?

Solomon, here, addressed a good name as an indication of character, not necessarily in the literal sense, as in what one is called. I get the difference.

But biblical names did mirror certain aspects of character, making those two concepts more equitable, such as when Jesus renamed Simon to Peter (the Rock). I suppose Jesus, as the Rabbi, wanted Peter, as His student, to grasp the full potential of his good name. He imagined aspects of Peter's character—sturdy, solid, immovable—before they were true. Almost as if He were speaking them into existence with a good verbal nudge.

Think how that impacted Peter when the rooster crowed three times. Surely, in Peter's failure, he clung to the idea of the man Jesus believed he could be, as opposed to who the errors of his ways revealed him to be in those deeply regrettable moments. In his grief, no doubt, he hung on to the idea of that name. Peter. The Rock. Jesus saw Peter as steady and strong, even before Peter was those things. It's a good lesson for us in the midst of our own deeply regrettable moments.

The ancient world was a respecter of words that wrapped one's character in a cloak of distinction, much like Joseph's coat of many colors distinguished him. Like who you were on the inside, your good name, your integrity, could polish the nameplate you were carrying around on the outside and give that group of letters value and luster. Illuminate them and make them shine.

But either way, literal or metaphorical, what's that got to do with my broken heart?

Grab a cup of coffee—and a blueberry muffin top out of the freezer—and let's start at the beginning, our beginning. Hang in there. The end is worth the wait.

———

Before most babies are born, parents obsess over what name will sound symphonic paired with the family name.

Studiously, they peruse lists of perennially popular names (James or Mary), searching ancestry records (Cecil or Charlotte), studying history of favored eras or literature (Romeo or Juliet), flipping through celebrity magazines (Apple or Blue Ivy), quizzing grandparents (Anna Mabel or Melvin), and even stalking mothers at Target to ask the name of the baby sleeping in the stroller (None of Your Business).

Many couples admit to discussing children's names on first or second dates. We're hardwired with the gravity of this choice that we recognize will last a lifetime, carrying connections of personal history and, perhaps, pregnant with future possibilities.

Parents possess two constants connected to naming: authority and relationship. They alone exercise power over their newborns, ideally in the child's best interests, with the goal of investing deeply in their care and well-being. It is an intimate trust that begins with the name. We imagine the best future attached to this title, dreaming of how it would echo at a baptism, a bris, a graduation ceremony, or engraved on a wedding invitation.

We see this idea of authority and relationship being illustrated early on in the Bible's beginning when God tasked Adam with naming the animals roaming through the garden. Clearly, Adam held the authority (aka dominion) over these living creatures, and their care would be expected as integral to Adam's charge of stewardship over the earth. This first man's intimate relationship with the Creator ensured that care for all the living things in creation. As that caretaker, Adam had the authority and relationship to grant the names. "The man gave names to all the livestock, the birds in the sky and all the wild animals" (Genesis 2:20).

That whole naming scenario weighs heavily on my imagination. I think it would be fun at first, like, "Oh, look at that yellow one with that ridiculously long neck and that silly thing that rolls into a ball with needles sticking out of it, and ooh—this one's fur is so soft."

But just like smelling perfume samples at the cosmetics counter, after about ten, I would be finished—even with the jar of coffee beans.

Somehow, Adam got the job done.

I think I would have caved and defaulted to A, B, C, A1, B1, C1, some sort of mindlessly rote alphabetical system.

With baby humans, though, it's different. Everybody loves birth names at the start. Or at least, they pretend to like them, because any smart adult knows that you keep your mouth shut when it comes to babies and their names, habits, and hairstyles.

I have to admit, when I entered the birthing suite of my sixth grandchild, I was thrown for a loop. I hadn't been privy to his name, and when I glanced at the whiteboard announcing it, I required a moment or two. "Tigris Wolfgang Timmons Holiday." I wanted to write "Esquire" at the end or "the Honorable" at the beginning, but the nurse had not left the dry-erase pen. I couldn't help but wonder—silently, I might add—what I would call this little man with the big name.

Tig. That's what it is and it suits him to a tee.

But this is what my son explained about choosing this name. "The Tigris and Euphrates were the two rivers most associated with running through the garden of Eden. That place, and those rivers, represented the world God created for us. I want my son to live a life that contributes to *that* world—the intended one, not the fallen one."

A most intentional naming.

Embodied in that declaration was a call for his son to engage and contribute to a better world for the common good. Just as the blessing of strength of convictions had been bestowed upon my first grandchildren, twins, with the middle names of James and John after the Sons of Thunder, and sweet Shiloh Reign, a delightful surprise of a granddaughter, whose mom and dad wanted her to understand her royal standing as a daughter of the King.

The names we give our children still embody the longings and hopes we hold for them.

It doesn't take much time, though, to go from blessing to broken.

If you think of grade school, can you instantly recall names given to us openly by our peers and not so openly by our circumstances?

Some nicknames can be kind, surely, but usually they linger longer when they are not.

Four-eyes.

Dumbo.

Chubby. Tubby. Tank.

Skinny.

Stupid.

And other slurs too tawdry to print.

And the not-so-obvious ones that label us "less than" in different ways.

Oh, you're in that *reading group.*

So you're going to stay out of class for speech therapy now.

These are ones to which I can attach familiar faces from my classes, even after decades. Horribly, it wasn't a list difficult to construct. It makes my heart hurt.

We all remember tags tied to people—and tied to us, perhaps—in our earliest elementary days.

Then we grow up and do the same thing all over again. Except maybe we're better at it, giving those nicknames to people who we've identified as not being part of our group, which we have so carefully curated. Where names were given to us by our parents to distinguish us in the best possible ways, names smeared on us as adults can work to distinguish us in the worst possible terms.

It's easy to do so in this age of social media, where epitaphs can be hurled with abandon, hiding behind screen names and emojis and cheered on by others who jump in with the pack. It's so comfortable—and cowardly—to virtually dogpile when not in someone's actual presence. We feel empowered and clever behind our keyboards, pushing people to the margins with our words.

Jesus modeled the gospel attitude toward the "edge-piece

people," those who've been pushed to the margins and feel like they are displaced from larger society, which is exactly how we feel when we are grieving. We feel separated from the herd, from the "normal" people, and even when we are not the perpetrators of our grief, we carry searing shame.

No scriptural standout could be closer to being deliberately pushed to the margins than Hagar. And who did the pushing? None other than the biblical heroine Sarai, yet to be Sarah. Not a good look for Sarai here. She was definitely prepping herself for a name change.

Let's remind ourselves of Abram's debacle in Genesis 16.

More scandalous than any telenovela, an infertile Sarai delivered her Egyptian slave, Hagar, into her husband's arms. For the record, that's never a good idea. After he impregnated her with "You shall name him Ishmael," Sarai and Hagar faced off, and Hagar fled into the desert, away from her mistress's jealousy and mistreatment.

Could have seen that one coming.

At a spring of refuge, Hagar gave God a name out of her distress. A pregnant and disgraced slave, Hagar remains the only person in the Old Testament who took that license. A desperate fugitive, she called God *El Roi*, "The God who sees me."

"She gave this name to the LORD who spoke to her: 'You are the God who sees me,' for she said, 'I have now seen the One who sees me'" (v. 13).

Again, God used the marginalized to remind us that the disenfranchised are precious to Him. Actually, esteemed by Him. They are the ones to whom He gave remarkable privilege, as in this case, with Hagar appointing a new name to her Rescuer. That in itself is remarkable, as the Hebrew name for God was considered unutterable because it was considered too holy to speak.

Hagar reminded us that God repurposes discarded things, including discarded people like her.

Like me.

Perhaps like you.

When we grieve, we may feel like foreign fugitives, fleeing our pain and landing in desert wastelands. We tend to name ourselves with the very things that are gone, overlaying our losses on top of our identity in yet one more way. These self-imposed names do the greatest harm, striking when our defenses are down. Like cutting, not to our arms, but to our souls.

Hagar had become Invisible. Banished. Lost.

As a divorcee, maybe Reject rings true. A job loss or financial tumble triggers Loser. A physical disability deserves Weakling or Cripple. When we suffer from trauma or depression, Crazy or Mental. As someone who has been betrayed, Fool.

We discount ourselves with such ease.

Somehow I can't picture any of those in the mouth of the angel Gabriel. They sound like their taste would be bitter.

Jane Marczewski, aka Nightbirde, a too-young cancer patient on the hit television show *America's Got Talent*, captured those concepts so well. Before her untimely death, she ignited the internet's imagination with her brave and bold statement: "I'm so much more than the bad things that happen to me."[2] I suspect that this statement resonated with more than a few.

You are more than the bad things that happened to you.
You are more than your failed relationship.
You are more than the number on the scale.
You are more than your bank account, bankruptcy, marital status, mistakes, and missteps.

You are not your anxiety, affair, abortion, or betrayal.
You are not your shame.
You are not sin, done by you or to you.
You are not your regrets, your sadness, or your broken heart.

Those are not your names.

Good names underscore the best that naming has to offer—a place in a family, a dream for our future, a shield against our failures, a blessing over our lives, an antidote for loss. Good names remind us that we reflect God's image and that we were created in His likeness.

Bad names strip us of all those things. That's why names matter.

What's this got to do with your broken heart?

Broken hearts are vulnerable because out of broken places seep sorrowful names and statements about ourselves. They seemingly rise up out of our pool of grief and float on the top of our subconscious until we skim them off the surface on a bad day. When we recognize that vulnerability, it is good and important to revisit the names that God has given us.

The following spiritual terms of endearment are declared over us—and I do like to picture myself as light as air, being held high in the arms of Jesus, toward the sky, not unlike Kunta Kinte. In these declarations, you will find your names.

So, God, who do You say that I am?

You say that I am

fearfully and wonderfully made (Psalm 139:14);

prepared for good works (Ephesians 2:10);

valuable—so valuable, in fact, that a priceless ransom has been
    paid for me (Mark 10:45);

worth dying for, and as a result, my life is worth living
    (1 Peter 1:18–19);

a child of Yours (Psalm 82:6, Romans 8:15, 1 John 3:1);

adopted by You, a King (Ephesians 1:5, 1 Peter 2:9);

a son, a daughter, but not only that, I am an heir to Your
    kingdom (Romans 8:14–17); and

sanctified, set apart, holy (Leviticus 20:26, 1 Corinthians 6:11).

These are your names. And more:

Justified—with a holy advocate who speaks for me (Romans 5:1,
     Galatians 2:16);
Pardoned, Set free, Without chains, (Isaiah 55:7, Colossians 2:14);
Precious as the rarest of gems (Isaiah 43:4, Deuteronomy 14:2);
Filled with Your Spirit, Sealed by this same Spirit
     (1 Corinthians 3:16, Revelation 7:3–4, 2 Corinthians 1:21–22);
Reconciled, Melded to You (Romans 5:10, Colossians 1:20–22);
Redeemed, Not wasted, Transformed (Ephesians 1:7,
     Colossians 1:13–14);
Salt and Light, I make a difference, Your presence in me defines
     and purifies (Matthew 5:13–16);
Kept under Your wing, in the cleft of a rock and in the palm of
     Your hand (Psalm 91:4, Exodus 33:21–23);
Desired (1 John 4:9–10, 19);
Seen, Known, and Loved (Lamentations 3:22–23, Isaiah 54:10,
     Psalm 86:15, Ephesians 3:18–19).

And lest we forget: *called by name.* This verse stops me in my
tracks.
     "I have called you by name; you are mine" (Isaiah 43:1 NLT).
     I am His!
     Can you speak those words aloud and feel the other diminishing
names being buried under the power of His promises?
     Speaking aloud holds potency—a punch. This is not a new idea to
us. We all know, for instance, the capacity of the tongue to do harm.

With the tongue we praise our Lord and Father, and with it we
curse human beings, who have been made in God's likeness. Out
of the same mouth come praise and cursing. My brothers and sisters, this should not be. Can both fresh water and salt water flow

from the same spring? My brothers and sisters, can a fig tree bear olives, or a grapevine bear figs? Neither can a salt spring produce fresh water. (James 3:9–12)

But there is a different way.

To speak scriptural promises about our value, in the midst of recognizing our need for repair, sets the foundation of a new identity. What redirect might it give to our internal dialogue?

> The same tongue that acts as a rudder to steer us into churning and dangerous currents can likewise speak good to our souls and direct us to calmer waters.

The same tongue that acts as a rudder to steer us into churning and dangerous currents can likewise speak good to our souls and direct us to calmer waters. Try pronouncing that list of words over yourself daily, which will act as a set of oars to row you to peaceful shores.

When resources are scarce, you may only have your words at times. But these words can be powerful and effective.

"The words of the reckless pierce like swords, but the tongue of the wise brings healing" (Proverbs 12:18).

You can jump-start healing here and in this way.

Let's revisit God's words over us in their fullness.

> But Zion said, "The LORD has forsaken me,
> the Lord has forgotten me."

> "Can a mother forget the baby at her breast
> and have no compassion on the child she has borne?
> Though she may forget,
> I will not forget you!

See, I have engraved you on the palms of my hands;
your walls are ever before me."

(ISAIAH 49:14–16)

God will never forget you. He will always wear your name as part of Him. He is a place of shelter and security for you, and holds you behind impenetrable walls.

And then there's this gem:

Are your ears awake? Listen. Listen to the Wind Words, the Spirit blowing through the churches. I'll give the sacred manna to every conqueror; I'll also give a clear, smooth stone inscribed with your new name, your secret new name. (Revelation 2:17 MSG)

For someone who relishes the fantasy genre in the world of literature, this speaks my love language. I adore *The Wind in the Willows* and the Lord of the Rings and the Chronicles of Narnia series. If I had a bucket list, a visit to director Peter Jackson's New Zealand *Hobbit* set would sit at the top of it. Just saying the name Bilbo Baggins makes me smile.

And then I read this passage—smooth stones, secret names, wind words, sacred manna. Any part of Scripture replete with such mysterious imagery fills my heart with wonder, my mind with awe, and my imagination with symbolism that sings. The clear or white rock alone, upon which our new name will be scribed, suggests the ancient act of casting a vote of innocence, purity, and, listen to this: safe passage. You can travel this journey of healing without blame or condemnation *for your imperfections*.

What might your new name be?

Consider this list of truths inherent in the gift of your new name.

It will be custom-made.

Distinctive.

103

Exclusive.

Premeditated.

It will give you access to a new and better life. Firmly fix you within your heavenly family. Remind you of your true family's name, rooting you to our Father.

It will proclaim your innocence.

It will be sacred—your shield—worth celebrating.

It will accurately represent who you are on the inside, holding promise and power.

It will be engraved on a rock.

It will endure.

God sees your new name much like He saw Peter's—a picture of who you are before you even accept it yourself. It will tell your story in advance.

It will be who God says you are.

Your prayer for today:

> *God, help me hear who You say I am. Your voice, Your words, Your name for me. Help me peel away the diminishing names I have imagined for myself and taken as my own. They do not belong to me. You have erased those old labels and are fashioning new ones for me, even through my pain. You alone hold the authority to call me and love me with the intimate relationship of a good Father. With You I am pure, innocent, free, and safe. You see me with all my weaknesses and love me still. Help me be what You envision for me. Help me embrace my new name. And most of all, help me remember that I am Yours, amen.*

Blueberry Muffin Tops

Am I the only one who buys a muffin just for the "top"? I peel it off and toss
the rest. Lovers of that crusty first slice of bread from a French boule or the
end cut of the prime rib, take note. Muffin tops may be your new jam. Bake
in a muffin-top pan or on a baking sheet lined with parchment or a silicone
baking mat. Wrap and freeze individually for quick access!

MUFFINS

6 tablespoons unsalted butter,
melted

1/3 cup whole milk or buttermilk

1 large egg

1 large egg yolk

1 teaspoon vanilla extract

1 1/2 cups all-purpose flour

3/4 cup sugar (preferably baking
sugar)

1 1/2 teaspoons baking powder

3/4 teaspoon salt

2 cups (12 ounces) fresh
blueberries

TOPPING

3 tablespoons chilled butter, cut
into small pieces

1/2 cup all-purpose flour

3 1/2 tablespoons sugar
(crystallized sugar is nice here)

DIRECTIONS

1. Preheat the oven to 375 degrees.
2. Grease the muffin-top tins. If you don't have muffin-top pans, line a
   baking sheet with parchment paper or a silicone baking mat.

3. Place the melted butter in a medium bowl and gradually whisk in milk, whole egg and yolk, and vanilla until well combined.

4. In a large bowl combine the flour, sugar, baking powder, and salt and whisk to mix.

5. Add the milk mixture to the flour mixture and stir just until combined. Don't overmix. Fold in blueberries gently.

6. Divide the batter evenly between the muffin-top tins. If you are using a baking sheet, spoon out small mounds approximately 4 inches wide and about 2 inches apart. The batter will be thick. I use an ice cream scoop to fill the tins or make the mounds.

7. To make the topping, place the butter, flour, and sugar in a small bowl. Use your cool hands (run them under cold water first, then dry them) to rub the ingredients together until crumbly. Sprinkle on top of the batter.

8. Bake 18 to 20 minutes or until golden. Let cool in pans for 15 minutes and then carefully remove.

9. Serve warm. They taste better when shared with a friend.

Makes 12 muffin tops.

CHAPTER 7

SEEK A SAFE HARBOR

Have you ever been at sea in a dense fog, when it seemed as if
a tangible white darkness shut you in, and the great ship, tense
and anxious, groped her way toward the shore with plummet and
sounding-line, and you waited with beating heart for something to
happen? I was like that ship before my education began, only I was
without compass or sounding-line, and had no way of knowing how
near the harbour was. "Light! give me light!" was the wordless cry
of my soul, and the light of love shone on me in that very hour.
—HELEN KELLER

I STOOD ON THE SHORES OF THE MEDITERRANEAN SEA AT THE SITE
of an ancient harbor, Caesarea Maritima—or Caesarea-by-the-Sea.
Built by the Bible's favorite villain, Herod the Great, it changed the
landscape with more than its impressive concrete breakwaters engi-
neered from volcanic ash mixed with seawater.

As horrible as Herod was, he did earn his name as one of the
greatest builders in ancient history, and clearly, this figured as one

of his crown jewels. The city of Caesarea, nestled next to the harbor, became the Roman governmental showplace on the sea and the direct waterway to Rome from the Middle East. Hence the way Paul sailed after being imprisoned for two years here.

As I viewed the gorgeous vistas, I recalled the conversion of Cornelius, the Roman centurion, which took place in Caesarea. In reading that narrative in Acts 10, Cornelius's courage and faith inspired me, but mainly it intrigued me. Gave me pause. What was with this guy? From what internal spring did his faith flow? What mystical lodestar pointed him true north?

To me, those questions, paired with a theologically rich, new doctrine of inclusion, earmark this New Testament chapter as a pivotal turning point in the message of Jesus. This gospel—the one Peter was chosen to deliver—was meant to enfold all humankind, not just Jews. Peter traveled to Caesarea explicitly to meet this Roman officer and to proclaim the good news for all, beyond the descendants of Abraham.

> At Caesarea there was a man named Cornelius, a centurion in what was known as the Italian Regiment. He and all his family were devout and God-fearing; he gave generously to those in need and prayed to God regularly. (Acts 10:1–2)

I pondered, *What was his household like, that this Hebrew God would take notice? And how do you shape a home like that, Lord?* (A book for another day.)

> Then Peter began to speak: "I now realize how true it is that God does not show favoritism but accepts men from every nation the one who fears him and does what is right." (vv. 34–35)

A timely verse for today if ever I heard one.

SEEK A SAFE HARBOR

"Surely no one can stand in the way of their being baptized with water. They have received the Holy Spirit just as we have." So he ordered that they be baptized in the name of Jesus Christ. Then they asked Peter to stay with them for a few days. (vv. 47–48)

I wondered how many Gentiles were baptized in these azure waters upon which I gazed. Perhaps they were baptized by Peter, an ironic and divine twist of Herod's intention for this archaeological masterpiece to heap more accolades onto *his* bloody throne. It was this harbor that drew the Roman legions here, Cornelius and his household among them.

Without the harbor, there's no city of Caesarea; without Caesarea, there's no Roman presence; without Roman presence, there's no Cornelius; and without Cornelius, Peter would not have been casting his net so wide as to include the "unclean" Gentiles— and that would be me.

God uses and usurps man's prideful intentions to sort His own plans. So, yes, you go ahead and build that harbor, Herod, and see how God uses it for His favor.

Harbors allowed places, and the people around them, to flourish. As a result, the teaching of Jesus flourished too.

What characteristics do harbors possess? What makes them so valuable? And ultimately, why do I suggest that safe harbors, or the idea of them, are important for our healing?

Check out this list.

Harbors

- are deep and roomy with space for negotiation.
- can be navigated without fear.
- are tidally stable, steadying in their effects.
- have regular currents with predictable movements that can be trusted.

- use aids or signposts, like lighthouses, buoys, and jetties, providing guardrails for forward movement.
- can deliver results, like fortification, supplies, and first aid.
- require dredging, which stirs the dirt but ultimately clears and cleans its passages.
- shelter and protect against rough seas.
- can be beautiful and, by definition, must be safe.

To get well—to be well—we need our own safe harbors that exhibit all those same characteristics: roomy and spacious for negotiation, steadying, predictable, protective, providing guardrails for moving forward, navigable without fear, fortifying, timely, lifesaving, dredging and cleansing at the same time, and, yes, beautiful.

But to rest within a safe harbor, we first have to be looking for one. Or, in the case of Helen Keller, in the opening excerpt from her book, waiting "with beating heart for something to happen," to rescue us from the feeling of being hopelessly lost at sea. Some sign, what *she* calls, ironically, "light," to guide us safely to shore.[1]

Her words—tense and anxious, groping my way, without compass or sounding-line—pretty well described me walking into the first meeting with my new therapist to sort through the trauma. I knew that my ship was sinking, mechanically going through the motions, but bumping into the buoys that reminded me I had no idea which way I was going.

Keller described it so elegantly as being buried by a dense fog shutting her in like a "tangible white darkness."[2] So all-encompassing that white becomes dark and dark becomes white. All the spectrum of colors swept together into a pit where a palpable fear and uncertainty crouched. In her blindness she *felt* the full array of all the colors, yet at the same time she felt the absence of all the colors too. Sensible and nonsensible all at once, everything and nothing held together simultaneously because the sensation of being lost proved just so penetrating and disorienting, like how my losses felt to me.

Remember, a sightless Helen Keller was not seeing this whiteness or darkness. She only had the capacity to feel them or perhaps to taste them; therefore, she expressed the emotion of bleakness as tangible—touchable.

I could relate to that. That's a tension that sets my teeth on edge. Like when you bite into something too tart and it makes your whole body shiver. One sense triggering another one that triggers a third one that has no direct connection with the initial ignition at all. An electrical circuit running amok, showering sparks in the most unpredictable places.

Perhaps that offers a rudimentary explanation of how mental stress and anxiety can produce detrimental effects on our physical health. Our bodies, through an involuntary chain of command, absorb the blows from the adrenaline-fueled thoughts that originate in our brains much like a driverless car that goes on a reckless rampage.

Sometimes, to compound that, there hovers yet another tension—a strange, reluctant tension that exists between desiring to get well and being terrified to get well. Some days we jump at the chance to embrace the new normal that God is carving for us, but other days we keep adjusting the rearview mirror, hoping that the old life changes lanes and catches up with us again.

I think back to the surreal moment when I spied a man on a California freeway without an intact rearview mirror. Crazily, he held up an unattached mirror with his right hand—freestyle—while the left hand gripped the steering wheel. Perhaps he wanted to choose what his eyes would see, instead of what safety—and his survival—necessitated he see. Unfortunately, that is a true story.

Separating your soul from those temporal things upon which you relied to shape your identity takes spiritual and emotional help from educated, trained, and trusted people who will guard your confidentiality. Those are the people lining the docks in your harbor, waiting to hop aboard and right the ship. We were not designed to heal in isolation, so lower the gangplank and let those who are skilled walk into your world.

I will unpack parts of my therapeutic journey in hopes of helping you choose wisely the professional resources to bring the secrets into the light, to understand the process by which we can borrow a cup of someone else's faith, and to break the bonds locking the halting first steps toward forgiveness, if that fits for you. Certainly, unforgiveness burrows itself into the wounds of deception and betrayal, if that is your story. Forgiveness, conversely, offers hedges against bitterness and its parasitic partners that can rob us of our emotional freedom.

Once I affixed my emotional rearview mirror and stopped adjusting it to look for that panel truck emblazoned with the words "Life As It Used to Be," I decided I would unearth any resource that would help me patch myself together.

I was afraid, for sure, but my "friends with stretchers" urged me forward—and maybe a few dragged me—and I realized the gangplank was packed with hefty resources. I simply needed to tap one on the shoulder and admit, "I need help." I practiced repeating that line, and when I couldn't untangle words to begin a conversation, I defaulted to that phrase time and again. This confession always proved a reliably good way to open a conversation. I told myself to say it and then sit there and wait to see what unfolded.

I sliced up professional resources into four pieces: spiritual, therapeutic, medical, and hodgepodge—a mess of stuff that doesn't fit elsewhere. These are broad, imprecise categories; sometimes your resources can qualify for more than one column. For instance, both of the therapists I saw held psychology and theology degrees—that's one of the reasons I chose them—so certainly they could fall into two lists. Just start brainstorming and drawing this out onto a page. It helps brush away the cobwebs to see it on paper.

The resource list at the end of this chapter is meant to function as a springboard. Remember, it is what worked for me, as opposed to an exact science for every person, and my hope is that it will spur you on to create your own individualized map toward restoration.

Even today, I can visualize an "in shock" me, shuffling into my pastor's office, slumping deeply into the chair in the corner, spitting out some staccato segments of my story, and hoping he would point me in the right direction. It felt like playing Pin the Tail on the Donkey at Rula Jorgensen's sixth birthday party, where I ran into the doorframe and earned an egg on my forehead. Needless to say, I was nowhere near the target. From that day on, I unashamedly cheated at that stupid donkey game by adjusting my blindfold. Except this time, in that church office, the blindfold wouldn't even allow me to cheat. I only saw a "tangible white darkness" and no target whatsoever.

That's when I first tried out the "I need help" thing. Without hesitation, the pastor handed me a paper with a licensed therapist's name and number. Church staff usually possess a "deep bench" or network of professional resources with which they've had a significant history.

I hobbled home and slumped into another chair in the corner and dialed the number.

"I need help," I said to the voice on the other end of the phone.

That's where I started, and I tried not to look back. But I did sometimes. Well, a lot actually in the beginning. And if I'm honest, I continued to look back for a long time. I knew that about me, though, and recognizing that problem, I taped the prettiest greeting card on my bathroom cabinet for me to see many times a day. It read, "She took a deep breath, declared her heart free, and thanked herself for being so patient with it." It charmed me and at the same time cajoled me into giving myself grace.

It doesn't hurt to hang these little reminders in conspicuous corners around the house.

So off I went, tucking my three saving words, "I need help," into my pocket or purse or inside my right shoe, where I keep my driver's license and dollar bills on long walks.

"I need help," I said to my therapist.

"I need help," I said to my internist.

"I need help," I said to my pastor.

"I need help," I said to the elder, who also was a financial planner; to the kind CPA who volunteered his time; to the small group in Celebrate Recovery; to the surgeon who offered, "There's something about you that doesn't look right." I said it to the guy at the bank with the picture of his wife and kids on his desk; to the "genius" at the computer store with the turquoise hair and an apple tattoo on his forearm.

"I need help."

I got really good at saying those three words. In time, the embarrassment faded and the humiliation slinked away with my pride, as I no longer set a place for them at my table. I discovered a new humility that sanded down my critical edges. I looked at people differently, wondering what their stories were and what hidden hurts might be tucked away in their right shoes. Ironically and strangely—as is often the case in the inverse universe of Jesus— the more I worked on myself, the more I considered others. I started to see a new woman emerge, like the legendary phoenix, except

> Ironically and strangely—as is often the case in the inverse universe of Jesus— the more I worked on myself, the more I considered others.

with a lot more groundedness and a lot fewer feathers. Well, truth be told, no feathers at all.

I continued to have bad dreams, though, and my daughter said to me one day, "Mom, you need to have the prayer team from church come pray with you at your house." Well, I had never been needy of such drastic measures before, but every defense was long ago dismantled and left out for the Monday trash pickup. And I did everything I could not to mentally sit curbside under the Trash Here sign too.

"Sure, honey. Send 'em over. Send Moses over with the serpent stick if it helps."

I made a loaf of my Aunt Dorothy's date nut bread, set out the coffee cups, and waited.

I imagined something kind of hocus-pocusy. But I was feeling rather desperate. I kept having this other repeating dream about a tree that had sprouted out of the top of my head with deep roots and wiry appendages that wrapped around the bones in my fingers and toes. Like a mash-up of *Jumanji*, *Grey's Anatomy*, and *Harry Potter*.

In the dream, I tried repeatedly, and unsuccessfully, to pull the tree out by gripping the trunk somewhere near my ever-present messy bun, but I couldn't budge it. I feared I would never be free of "it"—maybe you want to substitute your "it" here—unless I kept trying night after night. I awoke exhausted and related to Jacob wrestling the angel, except I was wrestling a maple or an oak. Definitely hardwood. It wasn't clear which type of tree, but it was gnarly and unforgiving.

Somewhere in the back of my mind, the phrase "bitter root" kept circulating. "See to it that no one falls short of the grace of God and that no *bitter root* grows up to cause trouble and defile many" (Hebrews 12:15, emphasis added).

The prayer team showed up, and I was delighted that they were two very normal women, nothing like the druids I had envisioned. Why, I could imagine meeting them for skinny lattes or Zumba on any given day. They spoke in regular tones—as opposed to saintly hushed ones—and it didn't appear that I was going to feel less spiritual because I was the "patient" that day. They were cool and smart and funny, and, oh yeah, very intuitive.

Okay. Let's do this, I remember thinking.

Understanding a bit of my story from my daughter, one woman, I'll call her Stephanie, calmly said, "It sounds like you're having trouble seeing your life apart from your husband, but he has made it clear that he's not coming back."

Understatement of the year, I thought.

"Why don't you just repeat this prayer after I say the words."

Phew. I don't have to think of a clever public prayer. That's a relief.

I got all the words out fine—something about breaking bonds or soul ties—repeating them verbatim, that is, until I came to the part of saying my husband's name. I just couldn't speak. I couldn't make it come out. I was tongue-tied, mute, my lips couldn't move. It was super weird.

I suddenly flashed back to Zechariah, who was struck soundless by the angel Gabriel because of his doubt. If you remember, Zechariah couldn't say a name either—the name of his son.

Could that be me? Was I doubting that I could ever free myself from this fractured relationship? Did I really doubt God's care for me? Doubt that He could use this "bad for good"? Suddenly, a thousand doubts danced in my head and conga-lined across the living room floor.

Stephanie waited. And waited some more. Three or four times she repeated that line.

Red-faced and flustered, not understanding what was happening to me, I blurted out, "I can't say it. It won't come out. I don't think I have enough faith."

It was then that Stephanie replied with something simple but life-altering.

Without blinking, she looked me squarely in the eyes and, with an effortless kindness, said, "Then you can borrow some of mine." Just as if I had told her I needed a few folding chairs for a barbecue I was having Saturday night.

I had never heard of such a thing. You mean, if I am lacking faith, someone else could loan me some of theirs? As ordinary as a neighbor knocking on my door and borrowing a cup of sugar? I flashed back again—this time to the healing of the paralytic on the mat. Scripture doesn't tell us anything about the paralytic's faith, even though he was the one in need of healing.

Hmmm.

Jesus only spoke about rewarding the faith of the friends carrying him.

Aaaah.

Right.

I was starting to feel like a Sunday school lesson come to life.

"Okay. I'll try."

Stephanie and her friend began, "Lord, use our faith."

I wasn't sure it would work—remember, I was the one with the empty pantry—and then a memory came to mind of the mustard seed necklace I used to wear when I was a child. That seed was so darn small. The one that reminded me of Matthew 17: "If you have faith as small as a mustard seed, you can say to this mountain, 'Move from here to there,' and it will move. Nothing will be impossible for you" (vv. 20–21).

"Okay. I'll try."

As if that exchange weren't enough, she suddenly added, "Wait. Let's try something else first."

Uh-oh. This must be the spooky medieval part.

I was not the least bit fearful, though. Rather, I felt comfortable and curious as could be, and I actually looked forward to what she had to say. It was like I was lunching with friends.

"I hear you've had some trouble sleeping. Can you tell me about that?"

I related the dream about the tree growing out of my head, driving *me* out of my head. It wasn't my number-one nightmare—that title clearly belonged to the devilish night terror described in chapter 1 where my face dissolves into a sea of sand—but I figured that getting rid of this one was like getting rid of my training wheels. First things first. My new friends both decided they'd go for a twofer and address that at the same time, doubling down on our requests.

Some simple words of prayer followed. I'm sure I heard certain words like *forgive* and others, too, that felt like sandpaper against my skin or shards of sharp, pointy things that stung upon speaking them. Actually, I believed that the words remained the least important parts, as I knew that the Holy Spirit was translating.

> I find a broken heart rather unable to contain deceit.

Remember that little talk from Jesus about the mouth speaking what the heart is full of? I trusted our motivations and the sincere hearts from which they came. I find a broken heart rather unable to contain deceit. I really wanted God to lead us, to use me for good, and to reshape me as a potter free to mold His creation. I understood that earthly pain was part of that process. What I needed was strength.

The phrasings weren't incantations, or accompanied by incense, candles, or tolling bells—not that those things are bad; I appreciate a good tolling bell on a gray day. It was just unencumbered. Simple. Childlike. Like it was no big deal. A request really familiar to the person to whom we were speaking.

Someone suggested, "Let's just sit here for a while."

In response to the solitude and minimalist sanctity of those moments, the "tangible white darkness" gave way to a word that floated up from the depths of a black pool, not unlike the words I used to see appear in the Magic 8 Ball that I played with as a kid. It sat there in my thoughts, like I had typed white Times New Roman text onto a black screen.

I confessed, "I am seeing this word, but I don't think it's really a word. I mean, I think it's a combination of a couple of words, but not a word on its own. I've never used that word. Maybe I made it up."

Stephanie's friend offered, "Well, I saw a dictionary over there. Why don't I look it up?"

Reading from the little brown dictionary I kept next to my keyboard, she repeated the definition: "Sexually unrestrained." Two simple words which carried a weight that was anything *but* simple.

"Oh!" I felt a sucker punch to the gut.

A picture emerged in my mind of me as a little girl seated between two men. I knew instantly what the symbolism represented. Sexual unrestraint had scared me as a child when a family friend repeatedly crossed all lines of propriety, and then again, sexual unrestraint expressed by infidelities had deeply hurt me as an adult in my marriage. For someone who doesn't claim to experience supernatural messaging or visions, this was really clear.

When she read the definition for *lascivious*, it succinctly fit into my story. In a CliffsNotes version.

What followed was interesting, to say the least. Cleansing. Much of it is personal, which I don't think is important to disclose, but I will say this. When we acknowledged that word—its interruptions, inclusions, and rude insertions into my life—and gave it to the Father to separate from me, I suddenly could complete the prayers that had evaded me before.

Just like Zechariah, my tongue was set free.

Not only that, but during that time when we sat in solitude, a vivid solution to the stubborn tree problem emerged. It seems laughable now, as the resolution was like, "Duh. Of course that's how God would handle it."

Again, in my mind's eye, a shining being appeared—Gabriel or a pal? This angelic courier carried a clear cup full of an amber fluid that was poured over my head, as if anointing me with oil. Flowing like honey, it coated the inside of my body, trickling down into the system of stubborn roots that reached into my extremities. I felt like I was viewing a celestial X-ray as I watched the tree's tendrils inside me being covered by the liquid. Then, voilà! The fluid simply dissolved what it had touched—not unlike the Alka Seltzer commercials where the tablets are dropped into the water, "plop-plop, fizz-fizz, oh what a relief it is." The roots? I dunno. They were just gone. Poof! And the tree branches, leaves, and canopy withered and went with them. All the pulling and tugging that had exhausted me and left me feeling like there was no other way, suddenly, a thing of the past.

> I suppose it's also safe to say that we don't often see our problems the way heaven does: Temporary. Seasonal. Redeemable.

Heaven never sees the problem the way we do: Inflexible. Unyielding. Permanent.

I suppose it's also safe to say that we don't often see our problems the way heaven does: Temporary. Seasonal. Redeemable.

That dream never returned. It had vanished in the night as if the Son had swept away the darkness in a word—or, in this case, in a pour.

You gotta go to Psalms at a time like this.

I turned to Psalm 37:4, to a verse I had taken as my own when I was a college student. It was engraved on a treasured bracelet of mine. This time, though, I started at the top of the chapter and this is what I read:

> Do not fret because of those who are evil
> or be envious of those who do wrong;
> *for like the grass they will soon wither,*
> *like green plants they will soon die away.*
>> (vv. 1–2, emphasis added)

I never noticed those opening verses before.

> Trust in the LORD and do good;
> dwell in the land and *enjoy safe pasture.*
>> (v. 3, emphasis added)

I think that "safe pasture" could be taken as "safe harbor" too.

> Take delight in the LORD,
> and he will give you the desires of your heart.

> Commit your way to the LORD;
> trust in him and he will do this:
> He will make your righteous reward shine like
>> the dawn,
> your vindication like the noonday sun. (vv. 4–6)

All after I had said, "Okay. I'll try. Maybe. We'll see," and had been open to receiving the gifts, promptings, and prayers of the people a loving Father had sent my way.

Be open. Be available. Be brave. And yes. It's okay to be wary. Uncertain. Thoughtful. Wise in your choices. But don't go it alone.

Your safe harbor is just around the bend.

RESOURCE LIST

In the beginning of my journey to process my grief, I jotted down everything I could think of that might be helpful. I applied the ones I could, when I could. This is not a complete list but could serve as a springboard to health for you.

Spiritual Resources

- Talk to a pastor at your church, even if you've never done that before now. Usually, there is a pastor assigned to a shepherding type of care, and it may not be the one who is the teaching pastor. Ask the pastor for trusted therapeutic referrals.
- Find a small group from your church. I recommend the same gender.
- Volunteer for church service to help others or in areas that you would enjoy serving. I served dinner at an Alpha course given by my church, which certainly didn't require a full brain and an intact heart. One of my favorite things was being in Christmas plays for the kids, and I played a mean Who for our church's *Grinch*. It brought out the silly in me, which had been on a long hiatus.
- Join a Celebrate Recovery weekly group, with smaller subgroups like DivorceCare. If your church doesn't host one, do an online search.
- GriefShare can help you locate local support groups as well (www.griefshare.org).
- Attend midweek Bible studies and Sunday services. I tried to be consistent so I could engage my brain in the series being taught. It allowed me to get out of my head.
- Attend fellowship and coffees with other believers to develop community. Make new friends who didn't know you and your "before."

- Keep your pastoral staff apprised of your situation and have them pray with you—and ask if there are specific prayer teams that could help.
- Search out financial seminars offered by churches, which usually can waive payment if there is a need.
- Sing and listen to hymns and worship music instead of the news on the radio.

Things to watch out for: I'm a big believer in gender-separate groups if you are experiencing rejection or abandonment issues, as you want to guard your heart against potential early-in-grief attachments. Give it time. If you are a woman, you never have to meet with a man by yourself. Meeting at a public place may allay any worries. If meeting at an office, ask if the door can remain open or if a second person can be present—for example, a friend you bring or a second staff member or pastor.

Therapeutic Resources

- Private one-on-one therapy sessions, as money permits—many professionals offer a sliding fee scale.
- Small groups hosted by your therapist, which are cost-effective or free.
- Podcasts, YouTube channels, or live online groups hosted by respected psychologists or marriage and family therapists (MFTs).
- New Life Ministries offers a free referral service and radio shows where you can listen to different therapists to determine a good match.[3]

Things to watch out for: Trust your gut. A healthy relationship with a therapist is really crucial. Rapport with this person is vital to good work. Don't hesitate to try a couple of recommendations before you commit. Ask if they offer free initial consultations.

Medical Resources

- If possible, schedule a complete physical. Tell your doctor what you're enduring so he or she can be aware of potential problems.
- Find an internist or family MD who can understand stress-related problems. I preferred a female doctor, but that's personal preference.
- Make—and keep—appointments with specialists based on your internist's recommendations.
- Commit to getting healthy with nutrition and exercise. Enlist the help of nutritionists and trainers, if only by watching online sources. Simple walking is a good place to start.
- Schedule necessary or elective surgeries and diagnostic procedures, enlisting the support of family and friends.
- Be intentional about being physically well, as much as that depends on you.

Things to watch out for: Stubborn pride. People go to doctors when they're sick, so don't feel like you need to have it all together before you see a doctor. That's akin to cleaning your house before the maid comes.

Other Resources

- Read nonfiction books with transferable wisdom. My mentor, Lysa TerKeurst, and Proverbs 31 Ministries are trusted sources.
- Attend women's events based on a commonality of loss or trauma, like grief groups for the death of a partner.
- Try self-care such as massage, facials, and mani-pedis as finances allow.
- Ask trusted friends if there are professionals who offer pro bono services for legal or financial matters.

Things to watch out for: Develop a trusted network of professionals, and make them aware of your needs. If they know that you are open to help, more resources can be enlisted.

Aunt Dorothy's Date Nut Bread

I once served this for a cooking class as a side to the main dish that I was teaching. I didn't include the recipe, but instead offered it as an extra accompaniment, sliced and slathered with fluffy cream cheese. I thought I was going to have a revolt. Once everyone tasted it, there was such a hue and cry about not having that recipe, they threatened to hunt down Aunt Dorothy themselves. Sheesh. Don't come between a woman and her date nut bread. Who knew?

INGREDIENTS

1 cup dates, finely chopped

1 cup lemon-lime soda

1 teaspoon baking soda

1 1/2 cups all-purpose flour

1 cup sugar

1/2 teaspoon salt

2 tablespoons butter, melted

1 teaspoon vanilla extract

1 egg, beaten

1/2 cup chopped walnuts (optional)

DIRECTIONS

1. Preheat the oven to 350 degrees. Grease and flour a 9-inch loaf pan.
2. In a small saucepan, combine the dates and lemon-lime soda and bring to a boil. Add the baking soda and set aside until cool.
3. In a medium bowl, sift together the flour, sugar, and salt. Add the cooled date mixture and stir to combine. Add the butter, vanilla, egg, and nuts if using. Mix well.

4. Scrape into the pan and bake for 1 hour. To check doneness, insert a toothpick in the center of the bread. Toothpick should come out clean.
5. Slice and serve with butter, cream cheese, or just plain.

Makes 1 loaf.

CHAPTER 8

NEW FRAMES, NEW GLASSES

Well, now you can.
—A WISE MAN NAMED JIM

WHEN MY BABY SISTER APPROACHED FIVE YEARS OLD, STANDING on the brink of the hallowed halls of kindergarten, the diagnosis of a "lazy eye" necessitated her wearing eyeglasses as a precursor to a future surgery.

That was back in the day when if you showed up to school sporting specs, a good dose of bullying on the grammar school playground was guaranteed to follow. Nowadays, there's sort of a status symbol of having cool designer fashion eyewear or blue-light-blocking lenses. With his white titanium Nike frames, one of my grandsons stands out as the envy of his baseball team. And I just responded to the chime on my phone, where three other of my grandkids messaged me with a pic of them flying to Hawaii, lined up like ducks in a row, each with formerly nerdy computer frames perched on their perky faces. The ones they bought with their own lemonade-bracelet-selling stand.

Yes. I said "lemonade-*bracelet* stand." My, how times have changed.

My baby sister, though, inhabited a different time. When lemonade stands were just that—places to ply and purvey your best seed-stocked, pulp-packed, hand-squeezed lemonade or even Kool-Aid, if you could get your mom to spring for that awful stuff that tasted so so good. And the currency was coin, not crypto or Venmo.

I remember that particular first day of kindergarten for her because our mom had employed the best of what I refer to as "baby psychology," that quick thinking-on-your-feet kind of parenting that meant you were totally winging it with your words. The key was that, in order for it to have a shred of believability, you had to posture yourself with complete certainty. It begged for your sagest wisdom, distilled from the experts like my mom listened to back then: the legendary pediatrician Dr. Spock or advice columnist Dear Abby or Mrs. DeBruin, the kindergarten teacher at Cowan Avenue Elementary School, who had guided the entirety of my parents' gaggle.

"Oh, honey, those little blue glasses look so pretty with your eyes," my mom purred.

"Mrs. DeBruin can't wait to see them."

And the most dangerous adage of all. "No one is even going to notice."

I knew we were skating on thin ice with that one.

Knock. Knock.

Enter Baby Sister's best friend, who figured to be the daily companion on her walk down the block to the DeBruin domain.

Although I was in the other room, I heard it all.

My mom's cheerful greeting, "Hi, Didi! Ready for your first day of school?" Didi was the five-year-old darling next door who had the mother-who-had-the-mother with the famous neighborhood

Grandma Cookie recipe. Which, if I'm calculating correctly, made Didi famous three times removed.

Halting childlike steps approached the front door.

Then, there it was. A moment of silence. A drop of delay before the inevitable.

"Oh, Laurie. You're wearing glasses," Didi said, with nary a nanosecond before she erupted in laughter. Giggles galore.

Baby Sister hotfooted it to her room where she remained self-sequestered the rest of the day as my mom rethought her baby psychology and regrouped for another sage stab on another day. As Laurie was her eighth born, I'm sure she remained nonchalant about a child missing her first day—or days—of school. By that time, she understood that it did not, in fact, set the trajectory for her future success in life or for a life of crime either. A bonus feature of having so many children and so few Instagram posts by other mothers who were parenting perfectly.

It just goes to show how insane it is that a tool like glasses, which will literally change your life for the better, falls short compared to the dreaded anticipation of how others might view you.

Now that part, I'm afraid, hasn't changed.

As you work yourself through grief, you will have to don new glasses. Glasses that will give you a shift in perspective and literally change your life for the better. But I'm not going to tell you that no one's going to notice. Because they will.

Some will stare for a minute and then muse, "Huh. She's got new glasses. Interesting," and then sip their vanilla lattes and go back to their phones. Others might size you up, think you're overindulging, perhaps changing too much, and discard your relationship. Then there are those who remark, "Oh, those blue glasses look so pretty with your eyes. I'll bet the world looks a whole lot clearer now."

The truth is, when raw grief moves in, it's almost impossible to maintain the familiar perspectives we once took for granted. A revised optical prescription is in order. Better frames with adjusted and updated lenses.

For instance, in the hard, early days of my separation, my sister would check in on me every morning and end the call with a newly coined, "Have a day!" We weren't anywhere in the ballpark of being able to chirp, "Have a *good* day!" Just slogging through the next eight hours seemed insurmountable. Having a good day was out of the question. A slight shift, but a significant first step. It might not be a perfect day, but it was coming like clockwork, and I might as well acknowledge its presence as authentically as I could.

Furthermore, we can reframe painful thoughts with time and intention. *I'm stupid* can become *I'm uninformed*. *I'm bad at this* can twist to *I'm new at this*. *I'm alone* can transform to *I'm alone now, so I'm able to pursue that goal I had years ago.*

Sitting with several family members who speak multiple languages, I commented that, in my younger days, I dreamed about becoming fluent in something other than English. I added that I just hadn't worked that into my life. It made me feel sad, like the opportunity had departed with my divorce.

My nephew, without hesitation, chimed in with a wise-beyond-his-years understanding of perspective shifts.

Smiling widely, he perked up and offered, "Well, now you can!" Where I saw it as bemoaning my fate, he saw it as redefining the possibilities.

"Yeah, you're right. I guess I can."

We both were looking at the same situation but with opposing perceptions. Kind of like the pictures that circulate on the internet where some people interpret the black-and-white image as a Grecian vase and someone else sees Elvis.

Dr. Guy Winch, an experienced clinical psychologist and author, shared his classic example of looking at a life experience with two different sets of glasses. Somewhat extreme, but you'll get the point.

> If you're a survivor of a horrible plane crash and you lost a limb in that plane crash, what is the story you have about that? Are you a horribly unfortunate person who became disabled in a plane crash? Or, are you the luckiest person alive because you're the only one who walked away?
>
> Those different perspectives are going to make you recover in very different ways, feel differently about yourself, and feel very differently about the life you go forward to lead.[1]

Single picture. Double insight. One view. Two outlooks. You get to choose.

"Well, now I can."

I can't tell you the number of times I whispered that to myself when I faced unfamiliar situations—repeating those words under my breath like a five-year-old girl headed to kindergarten with little blue glasses on my face.

What are some of your dearly held perspectives that could use a fresh viewpoint? A shift?

Start with your current belief: "I'm _____, so I can't _____."

Then try unsticking yourself by playing with the flip side.

Start again: "I'm _____, so now I _____."

For example: "I'm out of shape, so I can't work out" becomes "I'm out of shape, so I need to work out."

Or "I'm depressed so I can't be with people" flips to "I'm depressed so it's imperative I be with people"—of course, safe, trusted people.

Taking the time to flip-flop the disappointment into opportunity became second nature to me after reciting it a thousand times. The strange glasses had begun to feel not so strange, almost like they belonged.

———

One of my favorite gifts for someone experiencing a breakup is a journal. On the inside flap I simply write, "Well, now you can." That phrase suggests that this unfamiliar station in life at which you've arrived just might come with more than bad baggage. You might find yourself able to carry a large, red hatbox now, or a turquoise parakeet in a gilded cage, or a stunning rose-gold roller bag that wasn't possible when there were two of you.

I confess that it was helpful for me when I finally accepted that I was alone. Unmarried. A single sort.

Maybe you've finally accepted that physical limitation that alters your world or stared at the bottom line of your financial portfolio often enough to realize that you really are starting over. Whatever your new, revised normal, once you look it in the eyes and accept its presence, it somehow leaves you free to list the possibilities that this detour has summoned. Write down all those goals, dreams, or crazy, outlandish ideas that you once had entertained but were forced to table because they were perhaps unrealistic ideas in your former life.

Don't view them as limitations. View them as adventures, heretofore inaccessible. You might just see Elvis.

When I was deliberately choosing different words to describe my life—words that I had discovered hidden among the pages of fresh perspectives—I didn't realize that I was practicing something called *narrative psychology*. This swath of psychology uses the power of story to redirect an individual's perception of what might lie ahead. The belief is that the creation of a better story precedes positive changes in a person's life. As Professor Dan P. McAdams put it,

The growing body of research attests to the power of story in creating meaning in people's lives. For example, studies show that the most caring and productive adults in American society tend to construe their lives as narratives of redemption. These are stories in which suffering . . . personal suffering . . . ultimately leads the way toward an experience of positive outcomes and positive insights.[2]

I appreciate his conclusion, offered in this same talk: "It's really hard to change our basic traits. We would do well to work on our stories instead."

The power of the words within your story—the story you are now writing—and the vision it sparks are just too potent for our brains to ignore.

I love that Jesus loved stories and almost exclusively taught through parables. He understood their power and place in our hearts and minds. He understood that they could change us.

My fingers fly to Matthew 5. Jesus, sometime after the impromptu Water-to-Wine Launch Party for His public ministry, positioned Himself on a mountainside to deliver what some might consider His greatest lesson, or collection of lessons. He sat, taking the posture understood to be that of the teacher. He wore humility and kindness. The stage was set. The great multitude from Matthew 8:1 leaned forward, expectantly (my artistic license).

Might that crowd—presumably almost exclusively Jewish—have been looking toward that craggy platform, daydreaming about other rocky outposts from which other sermons had been delivered to God's people? Perhaps Exodus 19 and 20 came to mind, also a mountaintop telling, with God the Father speaking to Moses, His creation.

Moses hearing the voice of YAHWEH, "He Who Makes That Which Has Been Made," deliver the Law—the "old" perspective with which the ones sitting in front of Jesus have toiled for so long.

The Master Storyteller began. The crowd grew quiet. Jesus' first words confounded.

"Blessed are—"

He delivered what we've come to know as the Beatitudes. Declarations of blessedness. Favor. A deep, spiritual wellness pronounced over you. Blessed. Blessed. Eight times blessed. And to whom did He direct His narrative? The wealthy? The healthy? The wise? Those experiencing great blessings at the moment?

No. He looked out at the multitude and, knowing well each of their stories, saw the oppressed. Oppressed by grief. Oppressed by doubt and disease. Oppressed by shame and sickness. Oppressed by loneliness. Oppressed by lingering questions. Oppressed by hopelessness. Those stuck in a story that offers little hope.

"Blessed are—" A strange way to start with this crowd.

I wouldn't normally say that mourners are blessed. Or the meek. Or those deflated in spirit. Or questioners who want to know truth but can't quite seem to find it. Or those who choose to make peace when strife sits close or show mercy when revenge feels justified. I certainly wouldn't consider the persecuted blessed. The world would categorize these people with one word: *weak*.

Jesus knew differently.

What was He doing? He was redirecting the story for the hurting people sitting in front of Him who felt anything but blessed. Renaming expectations for their lot in life. Redeeming their narratives. Modeling new perspectives. Penning a new prescription for their nearsightedness. Replacing old, tired terms with refreshing ideas of what could be. Rewriting stories for the oppressed to become the redeemed.

Handing out new glasses.

Jesus, the Rabbi who chose a mountaintop podium from which to deliver the new perspective. A reframing of the way we are to live. The God-Man speaking new words directly to His creation, fit for the stunning viewpoint of the new kingdom. A marquee announcing a different season of longed-for offerings that satisfy emotional appetites and spiritual cravings.

In my simple, childlike understanding, this is what I think was happening.

> Jesus was telling people who don't think that "they are," that "they are."

Jesus was telling people who don't think that "they are," that "they are."

They are—and you are—well. Notice that He wasn't touting happiness here, which is dependent upon outside circumstances. Circumstances will rob you of happiness on a regular basis. But deep in your being, in your soul, you are well.

He was saying, *You are favored by Me. You are the ones with whom My kingdom will be built.*

That resonates.

You say, "I am broken."

He says, "I hear you, but I see your strengths underneath all those pieces, peeking through the cracks. The spaces in the brokenness allow them to be seen. They're hiding, but they're still there, and soon they will show themselves."

You say, "I'll never regain my footing."

He says, "With each day, I see you standing a little straighter and walking a bit more upright. I will direct your footfalls because you are looking up for My hand now."

You say, "I'm weak."

He says, "Today, maybe, but remember that you will find Me in your weakness."

You say, "I'll never be the same."

He says, "I don't want you to stay the same. I am constantly doing a good work in you."

You say, "It feels hopeless."

He says, "I know it does. I know your pain. But the winds will stop, the rain will dry, and one day soon you'll notice the sunshine on your face and remember how that felt when you were expectant. The warmth will remind you of My presence. Better days are coming."

You are blessed. Favored. Well. Those are the words of the kingdom, delivered to you just as surely as if you were part of the multitude on that very day, leaning forward, expectantly.

To every lowly situation, God says you are blessed. Favored by God. Imbued with divine purpose. Infused with hope for a different future. A pillar in His kingdom.

You may feel as if your life story has been erased and that loss has stolen its words, but we can all learn to write new chapters. It starts with reimagining our narrative to broker a brighter future, a future where you start with the words, "Now I can."

The power of words—and the visions they spark—are just too potent to ignore.

Grandma Cookies

This was a neighborhood staple on Beland Avenue, the tree-lined street in the suburb of Los Angeles where I grew up. Every important event was attended by a fresh basket of this biscotti (of course, we didn't call it biscotti back then, as we had no clue what that meant).

When my mom passed away at the age of ninety-eight, all her children gathered for a sharing of memories at her home, an hour's drive from that childhood place. There was a knock at the door, and our former next-door neighbors from Beland Avenue stood there with a huge plate of these lovelies. What a fitting tribute to the community that bound us all together back then and to the cookies that reminded us of how lucky we were to grow up in a time and place that recognized what it meant to be a real neighbor.

INGREDIENTS

1 cup (2 sticks) butter, softened

1 1/4 cups sugar

1 teaspoon vanilla extract

3 eggs

3 cups all-purpose flour

1/2 teaspoon baking powder

1/2 teaspoon fine salt

Ground cinnamon

DIRECTIONS

1. Preheat the oven to 350 degrees. Grease and flour a large baking sheet or line it with a silicone baking mat.

2. Place the butter in a large mixing bowl and beat with a mixer until

creamy and light in color. Add the sugar and blend. Add the vanilla and eggs and mix well.

3. In a medium bowl, sift together the flour, baking powder, and salt. Add to the butter mixture, mixing until combined.

4. Divide the dough in half and form two logs on the baking sheet about 2 to 3 inches wide. Pat the logs with your hands to shape. Sprinkle lightly with the cinnamon.

5. Bake for 30 minutes. Remove from the oven and let the cookie logs cool on the baking sheet for 5 minutes.

6. Turn the oven off. Slice the slightly cooled logs at an angle about 1/2-inch thick.

7. Place the cookies flat on the baking sheet and return them to the cooling oven. Remove the cookies from the oven after 10 minutes and let them cool completely. Store in an airtight container.

8. Alternatives: You can change up this basic biscotti recipe by adding toffee chips and chocolate chips, pistachios and dried cherries, or by using almond extract instead of vanilla extract and adding slivered almonds.

Makes about 2 dozen cookies.

CHAPTER 9

FOOD, GRIEF, AND OTHER DISTRACTIONS

Sweet company refreshes the soul and awakens our hearts with joy.
—James Herriot

"THREE WEEKS, TOPS."

That consensus felt universal in the beginning. That's how long all of us thought this whole COVID thing would last.

I was comfortably settled into the Montage Laguna Beach resort. So, yeah. Three weeks sounded about right. I mean, who cares about timelines when you're ensconced in those digs?

The world and its advancing invisible enemy seemed distanced by light-years.

Let me rephrase that earlier narrative, though. I was comfortably settled into the Montage Laguna Beach with a two-year-old and a six-month-old, tossing Goldfish crackers to the toddler between bottle-feeding the baby and stealing bites of my room service club sandwich. Is there anything better than a club sandwich under the silver dome of a room service cart? I was pulling Nana duty, but without complaint. I'll contentedly do that any day at a five-star resort curled into the coastline of the California Riviera.

"The kids," my son and his wife, were attending a business meeting where George W. Bush (number forty-three) was set to deliver the keynote. I was curious to hear their review—that is, after nighty-night lullabies, a candlelit bubble bath, and an under-the-covers read of the latest mystery I had scored in the neighborhood mini lending library. Big night.

The cherub-children cooed in the adjacent room, and the honor bar had been emptied of its chocolate-dipped almonds when mom and dad returned. From the balcony, I spied an executive helicopter, no doubt carrying the former commander-in-chief, lifting off and whirling away over the surf. I snatched the meet-and-greet photo of the kids and the forty-third president as soon as they tossed it onto the bed.

"Why are you standing so weird?" I asked, studying the picture.

"Oh, the Secret Service said 'No touching.' We kinda had to stand weird when we stood next to him. George was hilarious, by the way."

"Is that normal?"

"That a former president is hilarious?"

"No, I mean—normal to have no touching—like you couldn't brush his shoulder or his arm?"

"No. It's this virus thing, Mom."

"Wait. You call him George now?"

Yeah. Three weeks sounded about right.

I mean, George showed up, so it couldn't be that bad. Right?

The next day, California was locked down, locked up, and locked tight. As I dismounted from my spin bike at the gym, a fellow stunning silver sneaker-ette on the second bike over shrugged and wondered aloud to no one in particular, "I dunno. Do you get the feeling we probably shouldn't be here right now?" I bagged my padded seat cover and skidded away on my bike cleats lickety-split, with growing trepidation nipping at my heels.

Weird, all around. Not just in the meet-and-greet photo.

I suspect that a decade from now, maybe sooner, there will be scores of college classes dissecting the pandemic of 2020. From biology to business, economics to education, through the disciplines of sociology and psychology, the broad impact cannot be minimized. Hopefully, its legacy will leave us better equipped, informed, and prepared, but it no doubt also will leave us regretting some outcomes that changed us.

Certainly it will remain life-altering for my friend Patty, who lost her husband of more than forty years in the fleeting span of just three weeks. There it is again. Three weeks.

COVID's aftershocks will shake Patty and her children way beyond weeks—undeniably, for years to come. Her grief resides in seat 1A, at the front and center of its tragic aftermath. Her husband, my friend Driggs, will always be the face of the pandemic for me. That fact will always make me sad.

But sadness is not the outcome about which I am writing. Could there be more nuanced, less obvious outcomes that we ignore because they are not as plainly apparent as my friend Patty's loss? Simply stated, the collective grief of the pandemic mimicked the fallout of my personal grief. It picked the scab off a wound that hadn't quite healed to the point of leaving an indelible scar.

One problem that became painfully obvious was the damage that watching news nonstop, all day, every day can do to the mind and, by extension, to our emotional and physical health—especially detrimental because the day's reports were often digested in isolation. At first, like most everyone else I knew, I thought it would be over in those magical three weeks, so I propped myself in front of my screens and soaked up every word and image. In the early days of lockdown, the reels from Italy and New York proved traumatizing.

Three weeks of that steady diet changed me.

A general malaise stole its way into my day-to-day life, clinging to me like the glum-gray fog that cloaked the Pacific Coast in the month of June. The proverbial June Gloom coming into our homes to roost for a stay of far more than thirty days. I reminded myself of the need to interrupt the steady stream of bad news with premeditated distractions. Specifically, interruption with *healthy* distractions, sometimes referred to as *adaptive* distractions, as opposed to *maladaptive* ones—like not eating. I've tried that one too.

Looking back, I realize now that I intentionally had to walk my way out of that malaise. At first, as a possible derailment, I'd pick up my pink barbells and do simple sets of tricep exercises during the broadcasts, praying that I could keep my bingo arms at bay, although I felt guilty for wishing to achieve something so trivial in light of the rest of the world falling apart. I had grown accustomed to heaping on guilt or shame at every opportunity, though, and it piggybacks so reliably well onto depression and anxiety. This was the ideal season to perfect that pitiful practice. Why squander the opportunity?

Meanwhile, doing exercises while continuing to feed my brain bad news may have been helping my arms, but it wasn't helping me wrap those arms around a better outlook.

This had begun to feel familiar again, like active grieving.

Negative ruminations about how long I would need to be isolated and extrapolations of fears of being alone accompanied the news reports and lingered long after the television had been switched off. I even felt sad about finding the TV remote in exactly the right spot, because that reminded me that I had not been visited by my grandchildren, who routinely forget and abandon the control inside the snack drawer in the pantry, under the backyard trampoline, or behind the cushions on the couch. Crazy.

I longed to be rummaging through the fruit snacks for that lost remote, which would signal a return to the old, familiar normal. I wasn't prepared to be thrown into no-man's-land again.

Desperate to escape from the harmful ruminations and to awaken from my sad state of psychoslumber, I relied on what had previously worked to dispel the black clouds. I turned to those distractions that had helped me pre-pandemic, during the peak of my grief. These are the adaptive steps that I originally enlisted while dragging myself through the Valley of the Shadow. I realized that the pandemic had just allowed the demons hiding behind the cacti to rear their ugly heads again.

That dynamic reveals an oft-experienced and irritating part of grief. Sometimes new circumstances trigger old responses, and when they pop up, it's useful to remember how we manhandled them to the mat the first time.

This chapter could qualify as "intermediate grief dismantling," because in the early stages of grief, nothing tastes good, nothing looks interesting, and nothing can distract you. It's not going to be your first go-to when loss makes its debut. This is all business, pragmatic and practical stuff, requiring an objective stepping back from the initial steps that can be more emotionally rooted.

But once you've come out from under the covers, choosing active, engaging distractions, together with your new perspectives, will allow your brain to rest and recuperate from the hamster wheel that has been exhausting its inner gears. Your friends with stretchers can help with this, too, as they may offer ideas that hadn't occurred to you in your brain fog.

This brings to mind a verse from the New Testament letters. I recited it to my kids when they were teenagers, thinking, *Well, this is the time they really need it, with all those horrible rap lyrics.* Funny. I was the one desperate for it now, and I hadn't heard the bass and beat of 50 Cent's recordings for years. I was way past worries about Fif's impact.

Thankfully, Paul's wisdom runs those ruminations right outta town. Interesting that Philippians 4, the reference for that verse, is a chapter couched in his thoughts about anxiety and contentedness.

Finally, brothers and sisters, whatever is true, whatever is noble, whatever is right, whatever is pure, whatever is lovely, whatever is admirable—if anything is excellent or praiseworthy—think about such things. (Philippians 4:8)

I also love the translations that say "dwell on these things." Dwell. Hang out. Hunker down. Lean in. Reside. Snuggle up to the admirable, the lovely, the praiseworthy, the noble, the true.

Reminds me of an old song that's enjoyed several revivals. Originally performed in the forties by Bing Crosby and the Andrews Sisters, it was later recorded by the Queen of Soul herself, Aretha. It didn't die there, though, as Paul McCartney recently released it. Note: If you don't know who Bing Crosby is, I forgive you. But I can't help you if you don't know Aretha and Paul.

They've all crooned, "You've gotta accentuate the positive, eliminate the negative, and latch on to the affirmative."[1]

It's corny, for sure, but catchy at the same time. You've gotta love a song that starts with Big Band, meanders through Soul, and is picked up by Paul. It must hold some redeeming value.

But how do you start?

First of all, in the throes of grieving, depression, or the blues, contemplate turning off the news.

The not-lovely news. If you're streaming vivid details 24-7 about wars, rumors of wars, homicides, and hurricanes, it won't bolster your recovery from ruminations that run amok. If you're a news junkie and love current events—which I do—consider a break in the action while you heal, and try substituting screen time with music or a carefully curated podcast.

I have a verbal agreement with my Alexa device. When the blues threaten, she plays what I tell her. I am definitely the boss—until my grandkids change her name to Ziggy without telling me, and then I'm not. When I hear a song that makes me happy or transports me to another place, I add it to my antidepressant playlist. You'll find me in the kitchen, stamping my foot and ordering, "Alexa, get me my antidepressants."

I mean, who can listen to the score from *Out of Africa* and not imagine yourself in Kenya? Standing in your rugged Jeep on the savanna, like Washington crossing the Delaware, riding shotgun in your khaki shorts and pocketed white linen blouse, a Canon camera around your neck, and a hot wind blowing through your hair?

On my bad hair days, when I can't imagine anything blowing through my locks except my hairdresser's Conair, I switch to old hymns. If you've been sitting in pews your whole life, there will definitely be many that move you. My default hymn, "It Is Well with My Soul," sets my mind on a celestial plane. When I think of the backstory of its writing, on the wings of the author's inestimable personal tragedy, it redirects my thinking outward. It bends and blows my mind simultaneously. And my soul feels well.

We have a sacred charge to guard our hearts and minds. Negative input can come from the outside, like the news during the pandemic, and we can turn that off as needed. The negative coming from the inside, though, takes the work of the heart. More on this from Paul—the *other* Paul—in Philippians 4:

> Do not be anxious about anything, but in everything by prayer and pleading with thanksgiving let your requests be made known to God. And the peace of God, which surpasses all comprehension, will guard your hearts and minds in Christ Jesus. (Philippians 4:6–7 NASB)

As much as it's in our control, we should remove that which makes us anxious. Paul identified anxiety as blocking God's peace, and peace is exactly the thing that will guard our hearts and minds in Christ Jesus.

Second, let in the good. Choose something actively cognitive—something that makes your brain sit up and take notice. Engage your mind with helpful and hopeful ideas, intrigue, or positive problem-solving. What have you been curious about? What kind of questions do you google? What spurs wonder? What interest has God gifted to you that is uniquely yours? What pulls your mind from the spectators' stands and onto the playing field?

Chinese checkers or chess? Jigsaws or crosswords? Guitar or piano? Penning poetry? Painting or pickleball? Researching the history of Hollywood or Henry VIII? Couponing or crafting? Guitar, piano, glockenspiel? Writing scripts or stand-up? Memorizing Mark or Malachi? Tuscan wine making or sourdough bread baking?

Redesigning your bedroom?

Space planning your home office?

Preparing to climb Everest?

Mapping your fall leaves tour through Vermont?

Unsolved mysteries?

Magic tricks?

Tennis?

Badminton or basket weaving?

Baseball box scores or card collecting?

Calligraphy?

Can you think of anything more?

I dunno. Let your imagination soar.

Ah, there's another one. Build a kite and go fly it.

You don't have to become an expert in these things or go back to school for a degree—although you could. You just need your brain to take a five- or ten-minute detour whenever you find yourself getting locked into the mind games that send you spiraling down a darkened tunnel.

Imagine the distractions becoming the canary in the coal mine who will save you with her song—or save you before she stops singing.

Shortly after my separation, I decided that my youngest, college-aged son and I needed a mutual activity that would distract us from the chronic ache of our angst. Something that would mentally engage both of us. He was studying Greek on his laptop every night, reciting the audio prompts while I fell asleep on the couch. I quickly recognized that shouting "Opa" while banging on a tambourine was about the best I could muster with that language. I wondered what we could do together.

I browsed online and booked an acting class in the heart of Hollywood. Both of us shared a love for film and comedy and had dabbled in acting in another life.

Eureka! I found it. Advanced scene study. A class for "working actors" with a legendary teacher.

Oh my gosh. Can you imagine what this roomful of twenty-somethings thought when KC and his mom walked into the tiered classroom with the darkened stage? Who takes an LA acting class with their mother?

We won them over, those hipster people. KC, with his likability, talent, and razor-sharp wit, and me, with my snickerdoodles and what-have-I-got-to-lose willingness to tackle a romantic scene in front of my kid.

Ha! They think I'm so "over the hill." I showed them.

That Wednesday class provided belly-aching laughs, skyrocketing growth in personal courage (interspersed with flashes of terror), eye-rolling reams of notes on quirky, unforgettable characters to include in some future screenplay, and one other really, really unexpected treasure. In that class, my son met his future business partner. Out of this eclectic, unlikely, otherworldly, unplanned-for exercise in distracting ourselves from really, really unhappy moments, my son's life was forever changed for good. KC and this other student went on to build a wildly successful startup—a story for another day.

Look. I'm not suggesting that God's got a pot of gold waiting on the other side of that rainbow rising out of your watershed of tears. Whether or not that serendipity had ever happened, that really, really bad place in which I had landed was disrupted by this wacky, weekly, intentional interruption. It altered the trajectory of my thought patterns and, thereby, my future.

I read about a woman who, when she was going through her divorce, would bake cakes. Whenever she felt herself boarding the rumination train, she dug out her mixing bowls and preheated the oven, careful to follow every detail of the recipe. A successful cake business was born out of this distraction from her distress. I tried baking chocolate cakes for a while after I read this, but I found out that I like licking the beaters a little too much.

The exacting nature of pastry cheffing must be an effective tool to distract. Another example is Gwendolyn Rogers, owner of the Cake Bake Shop, a successful bakery and mail-order enterprise. Her "Oprah's Favorite Thing" chocolate mint cake sprung her to dizzying heights. She credits her success to the pleasant distraction from a tough childhood that baking offered.

> Her parents' divorce, her brother's early death, money worries that simmered for years. When she tells the whole story of Gwendolyn Rogers, it's clear she created a fantasy world inside her bakery because she needed one. She thinks most people do.[2]

What the above journalist referred to as her "fantasy world," I call her world of adaptive, healthy distraction.

As it did for Gwendolyn Rogers, cooking worked well as a distraction for me—especially soups, because when I was growing up, the cure for everything seemed to be a bowl of soup. Following someone else's step-by-step recipe granted my mind a reprieve from having to follow my own thoughts. This can lure us from our pain as we follow simple but distinct recipes that are specific and measured, a distraction that makes a good exercise to give our mind and body a break.

Stir this. *Good.*

Now whip that. *Great.*

Add a pinch here. *Okay. Done.*

Let me be clear. You don't have to cook to create a successful distraction. It's okay to prefer DoorDash or drive-throughs. I will say this though. If you do like cooking—or eating qualifies too—that particular distraction serves up a twofold reward. It opens the door to community—being with people around the table—and can function to make you feel useful again.

Grief often isolates, stealing the salve of relationships, and it's not always easy to manage what feels like the dizzying ride of social reentry.

> Grief often isolates, stealing the salve of relationships, and it's not always easy to manage what feels like the dizzying ride of social reentry.

It may be awkward to walk into a crowded party or a celebratory wedding, but sharing a meal with a few friends, on the other hand, might be a more easygoing entrée to that end.

Frozen pizzas are fine. Instant coffee works. I still love a toasted peanut butter sandwich (with mayo and lettuce—try it). Simple meals are sometimes the best.

Case in point. Forty years ago I sat at a table with seminary friends and one of their professors, who had invited us to dinner.

I can picture what the china plates looked like—they were rimmed in pink daisies—the endearing smile of our host, and the way he leaned forward when he asked a question and awaited your response. The meal itself? Unremarkable. I think it was store-bought soup with some sliced bread, and it had never been more appreciated. I felt so welcomed, so wanted, and so warmed on that chilly January night.

That is the memory that lingers, the conversation that clings, the friendship that "feels all the feels."

The hospitality message of the gospel? Just three words. *Invite others in.*

Community matters. Community heals. Community finds a home, first and foremost, around food and the table. Stories are shared, glasses are lifted, bodies are nourished, special occasions are celebrated, traditions are marked. Jesus and the writers of the New Testament affirmed hospitality as a calling to those who branded themselves Christ followers.

Maybe that was the lesson to be learned from the preschool ditty I memorized on Sundays.

> *Zacchaeus was a wee little man,*
> *And a wee little man was he.*
> *He climbed up in the sycamore tree for the Lord he wanted to see.*
> *"Zacchaeus, Zacchaeus, come down from there,*
> *Cause we're going to your house for tea."*
> (A PARAPHRASE OF LUKE 19:1–9)

I was a wee little wain when I sang that song, yet it seems like yesterday. Such a simple, childlike message to "invite others in." Timeless.

Apparently, Jesus liked surprising people with impromptu dinner parties . . . at their houses. I laughed out loud when I read His straightforward words to Zacchaeus, a chief tax collector: "Zacchaeus, come down immediately. I must stay at your house today" (Luke 19:5). No mincing words with Him.

The calling of Matthew, as one of Jesus' inner circle, is really indistinguishable from the call of hospitality: "Follow Me, Matthew."

Immediately after that invitation, it is written in Matthew 9:10 that the newest disciple hosted a dinner party where "sinners" dined with Jesus and His friends. Apparently the appetites between these two groups were also indistinguishable.

Interesting that it was Matthew who later recorded one of his Rabbi's most soul-searching parables, where Jesus tells of the king who was not fed or invited in, despite his needs. The listener complains, "Lord, when did we see you hungry or thirsty or a stranger or needing clothes or sick or in prison, and did not help you?" (Matthew 25:44).

Jesus' stunning reply cements the cornerstone of the gospel story: "Truly I tell you, whatever you did not do for one of the least of these, you did not do for me" (v. 45).

When you are grieving, you become one of the least, and when you feed, clothe, or care for "the least," you are fulfilling the calling that Jesus has set before us.

Fluffernutter sandwich or pastrami on pumpernickel. Period.

Jesus often did life around the table.

He used food metaphorically: "I am the bread of life" (John 6:35). "You are the salt of the earth" (Matthew 5:13).

He modeled behavior around it—blessing the meal and the Last Supper.

He made miracles related to it—creating wine and multiplying loaves and fishes.

He taught around it—Mary perfuming His feet while He

reclined at the table, and His penchant for dining with undesirables.

It gives us pause to consider how integral food was to His ministry and begs us to ask how it might fit into our grief-filled narrative.

Sometimes I daydream about where Jesus would be hanging out if He were here in the flesh today. I instantly imagine Him laughing at a table, sharing more stories while He shared a meal. He wouldn't care if it was homemade or delivered by Uber Eats, but He would care very much about the hearts of the people with whom He was dining. And we'd probably need to set an extra place for the Uber driver, who would, naturally, be invited in.

———————

The pandemic brought the revival of sourdough bread making. Everyone, including me, was posting pictures of their crusty masterpieces—baked in cornmeal-dusted cast-iron pots. It remains one of life's great mysteries that these tangy gems, golden brown, steaming, and smeared with butter, could simply be the product of flour, water, and salt. Jesus used all these elements in His parables. No doubt, we would hear them again.

Eight people around a table. My favorite way to share life. I think that was the root of my desire to start a cooking school that was about more than how something is made. It extended over to why it mattered.

Perhaps it matters most of all because when you provide for others or share a table, despite the fact that you are grieving, it does something very important. It makes you feel useful, purposeful, integrated, when maybe you haven't felt that for a while. Feeling needed remains a basic human tenet of mental health—my words, not from some academic, but learned from personal experience.

Take Nancy. The enigma.

Nancy teetered on my age range with an enviable head of curly strawberry hair. How else would I describe her? Intelligent, articulate, educated, and, yeah, that other thing—homeless. She, along with so many people on the street, traveled everywhere with a pet. I had gotten to know her, not well, but comfortably enough to ask her a question that I genuinely could not, for the life of me, process. Hence, the enigma.

"Nancy, I just have to ask you—the cat—help me understand."

I struggled to find the right socially acceptable, nonconfrontational, empathetically loaded, "I wanna be like Jesus" phrasing—and failed miserably. The words ran out the back door and cowered under the porch.

Nancy's eyes moistened as she answered the question I couldn't quite ask, "Why do I have a cat when I can't care for myself? Simple. She's the only living thing in the world that needs me."

Her reply hit me like the words of Matthew's parable must have slapped its hearers. I had expected her to say that she needed *it* for warmth, companionship, for someone to talk to. In fact, it was the opposite. It needed *her*, and she could offer it something. Something outside of herself.

Being needed helps wrest grief from our feelings of worthlessness and wrest worthlessness from the clutches of grief.

Feeling useful makes us feel whole, integral, purposeful.

Again, I didn't learn that from some study or therapy session or grad-school class. I learned it from Nancy, the homeless lady with the marmalade cat.

I thought of Nancy when viewing the TV adaptation of the sweet classic *All Creatures Great and Small*, tales of the country vet who roamed the Yorkshire

> Feeling useful makes us feel whole, integral, purposeful.

Dales to treat farmers and their critters alike. Great writing consistently prevails in the simplest of phrasing, whether it's penned by an ancient tax collector named Levi or a modern-day man with a love for horses and the hills of the English countryside.

This is one of my favorites, spoken by the main character, animal doctor James Herriot.

"Sweet company refreshes the soul and awakens our hearts with joy."[3]

True. Even if that company is a marmalade cat.

And especially if that company is a marmalade cat that needs you.

The hospitality message of the gospel confirms that it is healthy to dine with friends at the table where so much sharing can happen. "A cuppa with a blether" is what my Scottish friends say. And, I'm guessing, James Herriot would hasten to add: "And when you are grieving, it's important to do just that."

Snickerdoodles

I never met a snickerdoodle I didn't like. Neither has anyone else. These got me through some scary days, like scene study in an LA acting class. It can get you through some tough times, too, since it's hard to be sad while savoring a snickerdoodle. Win some friends with these.

INGREDIENTS

2 3/4 cups all-purpose flour

1 1/2 teaspoons cream of tartar

1 teaspoon baking soda

1 teaspoon salt

1 cup (2 sticks) unsalted butter, softened

1 3/4 cups sugar (I like baker's sugar), divided

2 eggs

2 teaspoons vanilla extract

2 teaspoons ground cinnamon

DIRECTIONS

1. In a medium mixing bowl, whisk together the flour, cream of tartar, baking soda, and salt.

2. In another medium mixing bowl, beat the butter with a mixer until creamy and light in color. Gradually add 1 1/2 cups of the sugar until well-combined. Beat in the eggs one at a time and when mixed well, add the vanilla extract.

3. Add the flour mixture to the butter mixture and blend well.

4. Cover the dough bowl and refrigerate for at least 2 hours.

5. When ready to bake the cookies, preheat the oven to 375 degrees.

SNICKERDOODLES

Line a baking sheet with parchment or a silicone baking mat. In a small bowl mix the remaining $1/4$ cup of sugar with the cinnamon. Adjust the cinnamon-sugar ratio according to your preference if desired.

6. Drop mounded tablespoonfuls of the chilled dough onto the baking sheet about 2 inches apart and sprinkle generously with the cinnamon-sugar mixture. I use a medium-size ice cream scoop for placing the dough onto the baking sheet.

7. Bake for 10 to 12 minutes. Repeat with the remaining dough.

Makes 2 dozen cookies.

CHAPTER 10

SMALL FAVORS, THIN SPACES

I have always depended on the kindness of strangers.
—Blanche DuBois (Tennessee Williams)

THE ELEVATOR DOOR SLID OPEN, AND AS IT DID, THE WARM WIND hit my face. I recall the smooth sound it made as it swept by me after the *ding!* announced the lobby level—smooth "like buttah." Reminiscent of the ball bearing drawers from the Helms Bakery truck on Mondays when, as a kid, I would hop aboard for the lemon jelly donuts. The drawer would glide out, smooth "like buttah," and the powdery sweet smell of yeast cakes, rolled in sugar, filled the cab. Those were sensations packed full of joyful anticipation. But that's where the similarity ended.

That's all I remember before my eyes responded by flooding with tears, which spilled over onto the floor. I watched them drop, and drip, and drop again more freely, and then dragged myself to the concrete bench outside of the medical building. There was something about the door opening to the outside world from the inside sterility of the doctor's office that reawakened within me the absurdity of the situation. How could it be, that I have walked so well the path called Straight and Narrow, but that I had just had my blood drawn for *that* test?

Sitting on that lonely bench, I was oblivious to those around me. Soon though, a woman came and silently sat down beside me. She took my hand and sat. Just simply, and without a word, lifted my hand, placed it in hers, and let it be. We waited there, hand in hand, as if she were a close childhood friend who knew what I was thinking before it was said, or a sister who could read my thoughts. Like a long-ago memory of ten-year-old Judy Bills and me, just hanging out, looking for the bus to take us downtown so we could perch on the stools at the Woolworth's counter and order our french fries and cokes—with a side of ketchup, please.

I never looked at her. Never spoke to her. I can't tell you her hair color or her ethnicity, or what age she was, and I would never be able to spot her on the street. After a while—I have no conception of how long—she patted my hand, placed it back on my knee, and walked away. I never could recall if she wore fancy jewelry or fine linen slacks and Chanel shoes or if she was dressed for sweeping floors in the offices on the overnight shift and was just leaving at the end of her workday. Those markers, upon which we so casually sort and shelf people into our idea of a proper pecking order, simply screamed, "Meaningless! Meaningless! . . . Utterly meaningless! Everything is meaningless" (Ecclesiastes 1:2).

For me, she was the angel Gabriel, highest of the heavenly hosts. It was one of the holiest moments of my life.

I call these *small favors in thin spaces*. And I believe that God gifts them to us in our grief.

I'm a sucker for tales of Irish mysteries where pious pilgrims float melodious tones through stained-glass cloisters in the middle of emerald green forests. As a result, I'm forever searching the internet for bucket list, travel-to-Narnia-like secret enclaves that sense the sacred, sandwiched between earth and eternity. The Celtic Christians referred to these as "thin spaces," where the distance between heaven and earth narrows, as if separated only by a gossamer veil, allowing us a glimpse of God's glory. A porous fragility exists in thin spaces. A little bit of heaven on earth, you might say.

I like to think the material world wanes at these times and in these corners, allowing the spiritual to rise large like a harvest moon. It awakens us to a timeline that travels—if I may borrow a phrase from the esteemed philosopher Buzz Lightyear—"to infinity and beyond," birthing a newborn perspective on our earthly troubles. Not minimizing them, but highlighting them. Knowing, for instance, that in the light of God's eternity, the scales of justice, skewed by the imbalances on earth, have suddenly righted.

The term "thin spaces" often would recall a place of particular beauty or wonder. For instance, Iona, off the coast of the craggy Scottish Highlands, usually tops that list. A tiny island with a big claim: the Benedictine abbey there is reported to be the cradle of Christianity in Scotland. The island of Patmos, in Greece, is another.

Goosebumps stand in solidarity with you inside the cave where John, "the disciple whom Jesus loved," translated the Spirit's promptings into the book of Revelation. How about waking to a crimson sunrise on the Sea of Galilee and watching a lone fisherman cast a net upon the water? Can you imagine the Sons of Thunder arguing on that shoreline, like two brothers would, about the best way to harvest their catch or whose turn it was to mend the tired netting?

Perhaps pondering Leonardo da Vinci's *Last Supper*, located in the refectory of the fifteenth-century church of Santa Maria delle Grazie in Milan, might move you. I think I would be beamed up to a thin place automatically—with a double espresso in hand—if I could rapidly recite "basilica di Santa Maria delle Grazie" with a passionate Milanese accent and appropriately expressive Italiano hand gestures.

While that may be the stuff of feature-length films, we can stumble upon all kinds of places—or even moments in time—where God surprises us with a serendipity, a small favor, reminding us of His care. Not only does serendipity encourage us, but when given the opportunity to share these small favors, it offers encouragement to others as well.

I believe that a thin place can be an experience. Purists of that concept may disagree, but anyone who has witnessed, wide-eyed, a baby's birth, or hovered on the hallowed ground of a loved one's deathbed, has sensed it. It's a blurring of the temporal and the eternal, a tissue wall built to breach. But what about all the dots between birth and death? Certainly there is room for thin spaces to sneak between the pages of our decades and days.

There are no biblical references for thin spaces. There are oodles, though, for hope and healing, care and comfort, and awe and adoration for God's creation. I like to think that thin spaces are a blend of all these—like the taste of a complex *au jus* sauce whose sum far, far exceeds its parts. After searing that rib eye, if you take the pan juices alone, it's just flavorful oil. Try rosemary, thyme, and garlic by themselves and one flavor overwhelms the next. But sauté all of them in butter, add shallots and seasonings, and an entirely new flavor profile emerges because of the layering of ingredients. In my mind, thin spaces are layered experiences of the divine.

Take *place*, first of all. Sometimes, in our processing of grief, a special place comforts us. That stream running through the park, the cliff overlooking the blue Pacific, the top of that sycamore tree that I climbed when I wanted to sway in the leaves and wonder about the universe or about why my mom and dad had to argue when my

SMALL FAVORS, THIN SPACES

friends' parents did not. We are not talking about worshiping nature but about finding God in it.

Place soothes on its own, needing no other accoutrement. For me, the hills of Tennessee and the saturated, seemingly endless rolling ocean of green, offer pools of emotional cooling. Add a ruggedly handsome oak with the fireflies swirling in the early summer twilight, and I can find myself transported to a favorite Eudora Welty novel set in the South. I can briefly, then, escape for a respite from my storm. Traumatic life events beg for a "weekender thin space," brief, self-aware slots of time where you can temporarily pack away the pain in a compact overnight bag.

I also feel the same peace in the middle of Manhattan when New York blankets itself in a comforter of white batting, softening sounds and stopping seconds while the most colossal snowflakes I've ever seen drift and pile up on the street corners. Mittened hands dusting icy crystals off my eyelashes make me feel like a kid again. Like the freedom felt in childhood's innocence *might be—could be*—touched again, if even for ten minutes.

Blooming jacaranda trees do it for me too.

When I walked my first grandbabies, twin boys—in that stubborn, behemoth stroller (but what could I expect for fifty dollars?)—I taught them a corny-but-catchy jingle. When we turned the corner onto that one street in my neighborhood, three voices could be heard sing-songing our way down the lane, "Every May and June, the jacarandas bloom." For two months, over two blocks, the pavement boasted a plush, velvety violet and lavender carpet, which we serenaded quite earnestly. I told the twins it was purple rain—thank you, Prince—and that God gave that shower of blossoms to us every spring so we would remember that He keeps His promises.

According to David, the author of the following psalm, we could expect that those trees would line up, burst out, and belt out every May and June.

Let the fields be jubilant, and everything in them;
let all the trees of the forest sing for joy.

(PSALM 96:12)

Or how about this version from *The Message*?

Let Wilderness turn cartwheels,
Animals, come dance,
Put every tree of the forest in the choir.

That makes me want to do cartwheels. (No, forget that I said that.) And who wouldn't pay good money to see giraffes tango?

I can still hear those squeaky toddler voices reciting that ditty. These days, years later, if I'm driving in my Jeep with the boys buckled in the back, and I turn the corner onto a street of purple rain, their instantaneous outburst of song carries me back to that thin space, where drinking in that beauty sustained me through some sad days.

"Every May and June, the jacarandas bloom."

"Ah. I remember, Lord. I remember how I felt when I lifted the boys into the stroller. Hollow. Empty. Hopeless. And then, when I saw Your handiwork and heard their *"ja-ca-WAN-das,"* You met me there. What a small but mighty favor. Oh, and thank You that I don't have to push that Buick of a stroller any more."

Find which geographic place fills your cup, and then go there. Often. And guzzle and gulp away with abandon.

Consider *people* as a second layer to season your spiritual senses. I have a friend, Debra, who possesses a knack for leading friends to thin spaces, like the secret lake in the middle of a regular-looking urban neighborhood, or the meandering walk along the bluff where you can count the sails from a hundred boats wrangling the wind.

Another friend and I climbed to the rooftop of a tropical hotel to lie on lounge chairs and view the midnight sky. It was an organized climb, I should add, as opposed to jimmying the window on the balcony and scampering up the fire escape under the cover of darkness. We gave that up years ago. Together, at 20.7984° North by 156.3319° West, we exulted in the stars that have the audacity to hide from us back home and debated aloud, musing, "How exactly do you think He hung them up there?"

> Look up into the heavens,
> Who created all the stars?
> He brings them out like an army, one after another,
> calling each by its name.
> Because of his great power and incomparable strength,
> not a single one is missing.
>
> (ISAIAH 40:26 NLT)

Does anyone else have to gasp for extra air when you read about the stars, "Not a single one is missing"? Whaaattttt?

All these slivers of spaces, especially when shared with a trusted companion, allow the Creator to speak to you in what I call "perspective poetry." Words that provide the proper place for us and our problems and the proper place for us to *put* our problems—with the Creator, the One who knew of them before we ever tasted their bitter fruit.

The psalmist scribed it so well.

> The heavens declare the glory of God;
> the skies proclaim the work of his hands.
>
> (PSALM 19:1)

> But ask the beasts, and they will teach you;
> the birds of the heavens, and they will tell you;
> or the bushes of the earth, and they will teach you;
> and the fish of the sea will declare to you.
> Who among all these does not know
> that the hand of the LORD has done this?
>
> (JOB 12:7–9 ESV)

Flavors adding layers. Layers adding flavors. Sprinkling the seasoning of Scripture over the longings of our heart. Redirecting them, when they too often errantly point us toward the bland and the bleak.

> Taste and see that the LORD is good.
>
> (PSALM 34:8)

Taste and see through the thin spaces. More specifically, taste and see through the *layers* of the thin spaces. Place. People. Perspective. And then, *prayer.*

I encourage you to ask boldly for God to grant you small favors in thin spaces. When your soul weighs a thousand pounds, and you cannot form words to pray for the grief that has frozen your faculties, you rely upon the wordless groans of the Holy Spirit to intercede. Dare to ask God for a small favor in these spaces. To heal. To lift up. To increase your faith.

> In the same way, the Spirit helps us in our weakness. We do not know what we ought to pray for, but the Spirit himself intercedes for us through wordless groans. And he who searches our hearts knows the mind of the Spirit, because the Spirit intercedes for God's people in accordance with the will of God. (Romans 8:26–27)

This is a promise of monumental proportions. If one of the

Godhead appeals to heaven's throne on our behalf, to speak in a language exclusively otherworldly, why not believe that this same extraordinary power can speak back to us in ways that are likewise otherworldly? The Holy Spirit is fluent in "Help me. I have no idea what to do" and will often deliver in the most unlikely ways.

Buck matched his name. He did not, however, match the clocks in his shop. A rather gruff, unlikely sort to be fiddling with fine antiques. More like the kind of guy who would be a tugboat captain or a cowboy wandering around a barn with a red-hot poker lying in wait for heretofore unbranded runaway cattle. Buck's shop was packed with beautiful specimens. European beauties, tall and refined, and American grandfathers, heavily chained with brass pendants and fine chimes. One of those clocks was mine, or at least used to be mine. A Scandinavian stunner, it had graced an oak-planked hallway covered in Persian rugs, and I loved it. It now stood silently in Buck's Clock Shoppe, wearing a tag with a price I couldn't recall.

Or at least I thought it did.

I sheepishly entered the showroom and sidled around the perimeter, searching for Helga or Anna Christine or Brigitta or whatever it was that I had once christened my clock.

"Need something?" the tugboat captain barked from the back.

I put a crumpled pink consignment memo on the counter.

Buck appeared. Thankfully, without a poker.

He straightened out the crumples, gave me a long, studied look, and a long, studied *hmmmm*.

"I was just wondering. My daughter's wedding is coming up, and I could use the extra funds. I was just wondering if you sold it. I mean, yet. I mean, is it still here?" Stammering, I think my voice cracked a bit.

"Well, let me see." He wandered back to the back, and suddenly I seemed so small. Shame was shrinking me, not unlike a favorite T-shirt I meant to hang-dry but tumbled on high heat for three hours by mistake. (I think I was making molasses cookies that day.)

Cowboy Buck returned—I could almost hear his spurs jangle—and, leaning on the counter, asked, "Where's _____?" Insert the name of my husband. Was I hallucinating? Or was he now wearing a sheriff's badge?

"He's gone," I croaked, barely audible.

"Funny thing. I just sold that clock."

Peeling off some Benjamins, he tapped the pile of bills, slid them my way, and with a final long, studied look, blessed me with the "Buck Benediction."

"Hey, kid, get on with your life."

It was then that I thought I spied her familiar profile in the corner—hanging back, as if she were in cahoots with the old cowboy behind the counter.

Small favors in thin spaces.

Buck's Clock Shoppe, not the Santa Maria delle Grazie.

Buck's Clock Shoppe, not the Via Dolorosa.

Buck's Clock Shoppe, not the Scottish Highlands, not the powerful Niagara Falls, not sitting shotgun on a helicopter banking over the knife-edged peaks of the Rockies.

God meets us where we are, with what we have—or don't have—and with our hands holding tightly to all our broken pieces.

Scattered throughout Scripture, symbols flag sanctified spots, like road signs indicating scenic lookouts.

"Thin Space Ahead 2 Miles."

Take Genesis 28. After a torturously restless night dreaming of angels hot-footing it up and down a ladder, Jacob commemorates the rock he used as his pillow.

SMALL FAVORS, THIN SPACES

For what it's worth, I don't get that rock-for-a-pillow thing either. Its name? "Beth-el," House of God. He threw a few more stones on top of that extra-firm headrest, so that it set apart the place where Jacob, fleeing from his brother Esau, received technicolor assurance of God's blessing. He didn't want that night, that dream, that place, to fade. He also wanted the generations to come to see the piled-rock altar as the symbol of God's bridge extended to humanity and a foreshadowing of freedom for His people.

Symbols endure.

Symbols empower.

Symbols express grief and embody longings.

In another era, in another part of the planet, Black slaves in the American South poignantly adopted this same symbolism in the melody of a stirring spiritual, "Jacob's Ladder." The plaintive pain in these strains, popularized in the soundtrack of Ken Burns's *The Civil War* documentaries, only hints at the despair of the slaves' captivity and the heavy burdens that bent their backs. Not unlike the dense weight of rocks and boulders heaped high in Bethel. Symbols like ladders connect history's cries to today's laments.

> God meets us where we are, with what we have—or don't have—and with our hands holding tightly to all our broken pieces.

The words of this African American slave song give us the vision of the captive passing the boulders of Bethel up the ladder where Jesus reaches out to lighten the load once and for all. Once past heaven's gates, there will be no *foreshadowing* of freedom. Only freedom. The real deal. Freedom will reign in eternity, the not-yet kingdom, to be sure, but as you read these words, it's not too soon to claim it as release from your captivity too.

We are climbing Jacob's ladder,
We are climbing Jacob's ladder,
We are climbing Jacob's ladder,
Soldiers of the cross.

Ev'ry round goes higher, higher,
Ev'ry round goes higher, higher,
Ev'ry round goes higher, higher,
Soldiers of the cross.

Children, do you love my Jesus?
Children, do you love my Jesus?
Children, do you love my Jesus?
Soldiers of the cross.

If you love Him, why not serve Him?
If you love Him, why not serve Him?
If you love Him, why not serve Him?
Soldiers of the cross.

Rise, shine, give God glory,
Rise, shine, give God glory,
Rise, shine, give God glory,
Soldiers of the cross.[1]

Symbols sear God's covenants into our consciousness.

Turn to Exodus 12:14. Moses built an altar of stones to commemorate God's contract with Israel. Again, so the memories of those forgetful Israelites would be jarred back into alignment with the promises of Yahweh.

My personal favorite is in Joshua 4:2–5. On the edge of the entry into the promised land, Joshua instructed each of the twelve tribes of Israel to choose one of their own to dig out a rock from the center of the waters they needed to cross. That seemed a bit outlandish, considering the currents were flowing fast and deep. But the priests shouldering the ark of the covenant marched in, and like the Red Sea forty years before, the waters parted. "Twelve chose twelve" and piled them onto the far bank.

Maybe you can choose one. Or two. Or twelve. Pick something in the middle of the deep waters you're enduring, dig it out, and start a stack. To remember your story. Because when you get to the other side of it, there will be more than muddy footprints to share.

Joshua, for one, wanted to leave more than his muddy footprints on the other side. He wanted a story to answer the questions of generations to come when the children asked, "Why are those stones stacked against one another in this particular place?" The stones don't carry any magic, but they do possess powerful imaging, declaring, "Child, I'm here. I am the God of providence and promise."

Rocks don't hold mystical powers. Jacaranda trees don't either. Concrete benches are just that. Concrete benches. I can tell you, though, that every time I pass a bench outside of a medical building, I smile. It's simply a symbol of the mystical bond that happened one day between two strangers, that allowed a kind soul to channel the reminder of God's presence in my life.

A small favor in a thin space.

Not unlike the Spirit tapping me on the shoulder and reassuringly whispering, "Child, I'm here. I am the God of providence and promise. And oh, hey, kid. Get on with your life."

Molasses Cookies

Originally inspired by my friend Debra, I have come to consider molasses and all the goodies that spring from it to be deep, dark comfort food. The kind of comfort food that seems necessary to sit beside me on an equally dark day when I need to feel some reliable goodness on the saucer next to my tea.

INGREDIENTS

8 tablespoons butter, softened

1/2 cup granulated sugar

1/2 cup firmly packed brown sugar

1 egg

1 teaspoon vanilla extract

1/2 cup dark molasses

2 1/2 cups all-purpose flour

1 teaspoon salt

1 teaspoon baking soda

2 teaspoons ground cinnamon

1/2 teaspoon ground black pepper

1/4 teaspoon ground cloves*

1/4 teaspoon ground allspice*

1/2 teaspoon ground ginger*

1/4 cup crystallized sugar

DIRECTIONS

1. Place the butter in a large mixing bowl and beat with a mixer until light and fluffy. Add the granulated and brown sugars, vanilla, and egg. Beat until combined.

2. In a medium bowl combine the flour, salt, baking soda, cinnamon, black pepper, cloves, allspice, and ginger. Whisk to combine.

3. Add the flour mixture to the butter mixture 1 cup at a time, mixing well after each addition. Refrigerate the dough for at least 1 hour.

4. Preheat the oven to 375 degrees. Line a baking sheet with parchment paper or a silicone baking mat. Using an ice cream scoop, scoop out the dough and form balls, then roll them in the crystallized sugar. Place the dough balls on the baking sheet 2 inches apart.

5. Bake for 9 minutes. Remove the cookies from the oven and let them cool on the baking sheet for 5 minutes, then transfer them to a rack to cool completely. The cookies will be soft when you remove them from the oven but will crisp up as they cool. Repeat with the remaining dough.

Makes 2 dozen cookies.

Cook's note: Substitute 1 teaspoon pumpkin pie spice for these individual spices.

CHAPTER 11

I'M OKAY WITH WHERE
I AM TODAY

*The person I once was is nowhere to be found, but
I've learned to embrace this new version of me.*
—Dr. Sheri Keffer

IN CASE YOU HADN'T NOTICED, EVERYONE HAS AN OPINION ABOUT
everything.

From what to dip your french fries in—ketchup or garlic aioli or,
Lord help you, nothing at all—to how best to lose weight—low-carb
or low-fat—to debates raging over e-books read on tablets versus old-
fashioned, hardbound volumes to hold in hand, to cryptocurrency
versus gold, to cats versus dogs. Shirt tucked or untucked. Pre-trib.
Post-trib. No-trib. Just throw out a topic and stand back.

And there will be opinions about you. And your progress. And
your decisions. And your choices.

Protect that progress by employing strategies to strengthen.

Be okay with where you are today. Start with that one.

Be patient with yourself. Healing isn't a bullet train streaking
across the landscape. It's also not like the Chunnel, with that reliable

high-speed London-to-Paris train sailing through the underbelly of the English Channel, seemingly unconcerned that somehow it bears the weight of 246 feet of earth above it—the equivalent distance of 107 baguettes balancing upon each other, the French would have you know.[1] Healing from loss looks less "express" and more like the lumbering steam engine at Disneyland that sometimes runs—very slowly and scenically—and sometimes posts signage announcing, "Closed for Repairs."

"Aren't you over it yet?" You'll get that one plenty of times. If not outright, in the condescending look that says it all without saying anything at all. That exact question came from my ex—especially effective in stoking the shame and spreading the doubt. Much like fertilizer, that stinks.

One doesn't "get over" grief. We learn to wrestle with it, grow in respect for its presence, and, in that process, reach a level of acceptance. "Sometimes we wait not for change, but for the grace to accept the status quo," or at least that's what writer Heidi Thomas scripted for one of my favorite characters in *Call the Midwife*.[2] For being fictional, they're sure smart.

Learning to set boundaries with people who think that you should be over it is an art form that requires a planned response, which is helpful to create *before* you need it.

This chapter will suggest some of those strategies. As you consider them, keep in mind that therapists will tell us that healing is a highly individualized process and that extrapolating too far into the future can be counterproductive. If you feel sheepish and cry, "But I should be further along," remember the kind words from a wise woman who told me, "It takes a long time to heal a broken heart."

We wound as individuals and heal as individuals. We all bring varying life experiences that set the scene for our grief, reminiscent of theatrical backdrops custom-designed for your very own play. The scenery is put into place, and your script played out with characters and music and props unique to you. Therefore, you can never measure your "success" or compare your "performance reviews" to anyone else's.

Let me say something here about what Dr. Paul Conti—in his book *Trauma: The Invisible Epidemic*—refers to as "multiple hits."[3] That's his term for successive incidents of trauma, which pile on until such time that these collective life experiences—this "context," this backdrop—intersect a loss that becomes the "last straw." I have referred to it in my own life as "an avalanche of loss."

It reminds me of CARFAX, the auto-buying service that tells you if the car you're interested in purchasing has ever been in an accident. It's billed simply as a "history impact tool." Cars can look shiny and new on the outside but may have sustained serious damage to the undercarriage, hidden from the eye. Those hidden histories can potentially predict future catastrophes.

When my mini SUV was rear-ended, it looked like nothing much had happened. The mechanic explained that it was totaled, though, as the chassis had folded onto itself, crimping, rendering it undriveable. He went on to say that even if it was repaired, the basic infrastructure of the car would remain weakened, and if hit again, would be vulnerable to an accordion-like collapse. Hence the value of the CARFAX. Once a car has been in an accident, the overall safety can be compromised, and with each successive hit, the damage is compounded—even if the successive hit was not as bad as the initial one.

I liken that to repeated incidents of infidelity, or negative multiple hits of any type. It may look unscathed. It may appear perfect. It's fine as long as there are no more insults. But with repeated traumatic events, the chassis is unable to hold itself together. The car, aka the relationship, gets hauled off to the junkyard.

For those of you who have sustained multiple hits, your restoration will be nothing like someone who is dealing with a single negative life event. No one can fully know what someone else's "theatrical backdrop" looks like, or how the "trauma fax"—your history impact report—reads, so there never should be anyone criticizing your journey. It is yours and yours alone. You don't have to accept the stigma that anyone else is trying to give you. Shed it.

A note here to add to the call to shed stigma: though we've come a long way in bringing mental and emotional health to the public forefront, there may be some lingering opinions that therapy is for "crazy" people. Criticism can come from all corners. There remain loud voices in the Christian community that tout not needing help other than what you can find in Scripture. Be wary of those who don't understand that a hurting heart has never been healed with theological debate.

> Be wary of those who don't understand that a hurting heart has never been healed with theological debate.

Nothing brings out the critics and debate teams faster than social media, so think twice about what you choose to share publicly. If in doubt about how much to share, go with the old design adage upon which I have relied for years: "less is more."

So what do you say to the person who offers an unsolicited opinion about your situation or ventures an unwelcomed query? Here are some sample questions and ideas for answers.

"AREN'T YOU OVER IT YET?"

"I'm not sure 'over it' is the right description. I'm processing things, and I'm really proud of my progress."

"Slow and steady wins the race."

"It's super important to me that I take my time to heal with intention. It's been hard but rewarding."

"I'd rather take my time with this and be patient with myself."

Offer some responses with a bit of your personality or humor. I might have said things like this:

"Right? It's a heck of a run, and I'll be doggone if I know where God's put that finish line!"

"I cannot lie. I'm hoping to be miserable for the rest of my days, and I hope you'll support me in that."

"When I figure out what 'over it' means, I'll get back to you."

"Over, under, through it, around it, beneath it—hmmm—I suppose as soon as I figure out how not to end sentences with a preposition, I will figure it out. Oops. There I go again."

I remember a talk show host grilling Martha Stewart about her divorce. It's telling that I have tucked this years-ago reply into the grooves of my memory bank.

With a gravelly tone the interviewer asked, "Are you over it yet?"—poking that cool-as-a-cucumber vibe Ms. Stewart wears so well.

Her instantaneous response shot back, "I don't know. Do you ever get over it?"

Right on, Martha. The night of that broadcast, I made a meatloaf in her honor, and inspired by her response to a prickly question, my girlfriends and I wrote out a script for me to memorize when I ran into old acquaintances who were more interested in gossip than in my well-being.

"HOW ARE YOU DOING?"

"Well. I've really taken the time to work on myself in a
   meaningful way."

"I'm enjoying life in new ways, and that's been really good."

"Hard stuff can also be good stuff. I'm learning lots. Thanks for
   asking."

"Things are different, but that's okay. New normals sometimes
   take time."

"I'm well. The kids and I are fine, and we find it works best to
   keep the personal stuff under our roof."

"Fantastic. I'm thinking this might be a good time to join the
   circus."

You can also follow up your reply with a simple redirect like,
"Oh, would ya look at that—buy five toilet paper rolls and the sixth is
free" or "Whaddya think about them Dodgers?" or a reliable "How're
things in your world?" Generally, people will jump at the chance to
tell you about themselves.

Scripting and role-playing are always good strategies, but you
may need to enlist sturdier ones.

Sometimes good fences make good neighbors. You don't have
to subject yourself to people who aren't trustworthy or don't have
your family's best interests in mind. Erect some boundaries to protect your healing and to ensure its continued growth. You don't have
to go into great detail to say no. Learn to give a succinct reply and
then stop talking. A smile and a "gotta go" can be an adequate exit.
As one therapist posting on Instagram wrote,

A boundary with yourself can look like sharing what you want
people to know and keeping the rest to yourself. You can share
when you're ready. You have a right to privacy even when people

are requesting more information. People do not have to under-stand your boundaries to honor them.[4]

Sometimes that means setting boundaries with family.

My mom, well into her nineties, never really understood my losses. I knew that her lack of sensitivity rested squarely with her diminishing cognitive function, but still, when she mockingly referred to me as her "poor little rich girl," it hurt. She had been the happy beneficiary of my former life, where a different financial standing had allowed her to enjoy some niceties. Now that I was struggling financially, she seemed to take a strange pleasure in that.

I learned to visit my mom with one of my sisters in tow or to keep it brief and upbeat, directing the conversation to her needs. I also had to mind my spiritual fortifications, praying for her peace, as I felt certain that this derision was not good for her soul either. I took encouragement in the fact that this was not the parent of my youth—a kind, fun, and attentive mom. I had grieved that mother long ago. It was God's unmerited favor toward me that allowed me to offer the same to her. It wasn't easy, though, if I'm honest.

Sometimes family won't be the ones to support you. That's when you rely upon your *hanai*.

Hanai is a beautiful word that my kids and I learned from some native Hawaiians on the island of Maui. In Polynesian historical cul-ture, if a woman was childless, the woman's sister would bear a child and present it to the infertile sibling as an adopted baby. This baby would be lovingly referred to as "the hanai," the adopted one. The chosen one. Considered the greatest of gifts.

We had traveled to the Hawaiian Islands to hold a beach memo-rial service for Sarah, since she had loved Maui more than any other place in the world. In a ceremony called a "paddle-out," from flower-strewn surfboards the family members scatter the loved one's ashes beyond the waves. Surrounded by fiery-orange hibiscus and purple-throated orchids near the Kaanapali Beach pathways where Sarah had strolled the now-grown-up kids as babies, the officiant listened to each of our stories about what Sarah meant to us. After hearing our words, he simply stated, "Sarah was your hanai, and you were hers." *Hanai*—the family you choose. *Hanai*—the family we chose for each other so many years ago.

It is good to have nonrelated friends whom we also informally adopt as family. Your hanai. Those who can share your deepest wounds and your loftiest dreams. Sarah definitely proved that to be true for me.

If you have one or two or a few loving family members who walk with you in this journey, you're doubly blessed. They can use their intimate knowledge to remind you that there will be a place for you in this unasked for, untried, newfangled life on the sunnier side of loss.

Learning to be okay with where you are today means recognizing that you aren't the same person anymore. Dr. Sheri Keffer, my therapist, described it like this: "The person I once was is nowhere to be found, but I've learned to embrace this new version of me."

> Learning to be okay with where you are today means recognizing that you aren't the same person anymore.

You've endured loss. You're figuring out how to reengage the world in unfamiliar ways with novel ways of thinking. Perhaps you're reflecting upon all you're learning in therapy, and you're discovering where you find support and where you need to install guardrails.

Again, I appreciate Dr. Conti's appraisal that "regardless of the nature or severity of the traumatic event, our before-and-after stories couldn't be more different."[5]

This also might be the time to take a breath and step outside while contemplating those differences. For me, this point in my healing begged for fresh air and space to breathe. Nowhere did I find that so useful as in taking long walks by myself.

It was in those walks that I started to notice the world again.

It's the stage where you might start noticing the world again too. Looking up and daring to allow slivers of wonder and imagination to mingle with your grief. It may be the first time you've asked your grief—or told it plainly—to move aside to make room for something else. It's the time when an emerging picture is being painted in small strokes, which might just allow your perceptions and profundities to guide those strokes into a meaningful portrait of the possible.

I'm praying for that very thing for you.

Not-Over-It-Yet Meatloaf

I used to think that meatloaf was boring and unappealing because of how ordinary it was. But when I took a leftover meatloaf sandwich to my histology class, stacked on nubby wheat bread with a layer of crisp lettuce and drizzled with chipotle mayo and honey mustard, I could've sold it for at least a day's worth of tuition. Of course, I said no. I savored every bite. And I got an A on my test that day. It's amazing what confidence a little "classmate envy" will produce.

For a variation, make mini-meatloaves in muffin tins. Sliced in half, the "muffin meatloaves" make dandy sandwiches on a bun. Freeze before or after baking.

INGREDIENTS

1 pound ground beef

1 pound ground pork

1 sweet onion, quartered

3 carrots, cut into 2-inch pieces

1/2 red or orange bell pepper, quartered

1/2 cup breadcrumbs

1 egg, beaten

1 tablespoon seasoned salt

1 teaspoon ground black pepper

1 cup ketchup, divided

2 tablespoons brown sugar

1 teaspoon dry mustard

1/2 onion, cut into rings and separated

DIRECTIONS

1. Preheat the oven to 350 degrees. Place a sheet of parchment paper over a wire rack and set the rack on top of a foil-lined jelly roll pan.
2. Place the beef and pork in a large mixing bowl.
3. Place the onion, carrots, and bell pepper in the bowl of a food processor and pulse until finely chopped. (Or chop the vegetables by hand.) Add the vegetables to the meat. Add the breadcrumbs, egg, salt, pepper, and ¼ cup of the ketchup. Mix well. (I use gloved hands to mix.)
4. Shape the meat mixture into one large loaf or two smaller loaves* and place on the rack. You can also bake them directly in a baking pan without the rack. Alternately, use a loaf pan or fill muffin tins.
5. In a small bowl combine the remaining ¾ cup ketchup, brown sugar, and dry mustard. Lay the separated onion rings on top of the loaves. Spoon the ketchup mixture on top.
6. Bake for 60 minutes if in muffin tins or 90 minutes if in a single loaf pan or on a rack.

Makes 8 servings.

*Cook's note: I prefer to make 2 (8-inch) loaves—one for dinner and one to stick in the fridge for sandwiches.

CHAPTER 12

CONTINUING EDUCATION

Truly I am your servant, Lord;
I serve you just as my mother did;
you have freed me from my chains.
—Psalm 116:16

WHEN I WAS A YOUNG MOM, I WAS A BIG FAN OF JIM TRELEASE, author of *The Read-Aloud Handbook*. His book had been gifted to me when I was pregnant with my firstborn by an especially resourceful friend of my mother's, whom I admired for her intelligence and creativity.

Attending a lecture by Trelease when my kids were elementary-school aged, I remember him recommending a children's classic, *Where the Red Fern Grows*. I sat up and took notice, since that had been one of my favorites too. Curled up on my big bed, reading it to my kids, there was no shortage of tears from my children or me when Billy's hound dog, Old Dan, sacrifices his life, protecting the young boy from a mountain lion. When Little Ann—spoiler alert—flops herself despondently on top of the grave of Old Dan, it's almost too much to bear. I was curious as to why, out of all the books, Trelease had spotlighted this one. It was beautifully written but so darn sad.

Trelease explained during the lecture that the beauty of a sad story is that it teaches children how to cry for others. His belief was that every baby enters the world instinctively knowing how to cry for themselves. The other trait—shedding tears for others—has to be learned.

I've never forgotten that. And although it wasn't a spiritual gathering, he certainly taught a spiritual concept Jesus would have lauded.

Tears came to Jesus too.

Of course, the example we all point to is at Lazarus's grave. I even remember having that discussion with my seventh-grade English teacher, Mr. Robert Jurkowski, who wore Hush Puppies and cool corduroy blazers with suede elbow patches. A handsome fella with dazzling white teeth, who had the Home Economics department abuzz and Miss Alice Kachigian and Miss Sally Edison at odds, he quizzed our class of awkward middle schoolers one day about that very account from the Bible. Striding through the aisles to the front of the room, he hollered to the blackboard, "Who can recite the shortest sentence in the English language?"

We all awkwardly hung our awkward heads in an awkward way, signaling that we weren't going to risk awkwardly shouting out the wrong answer.

"Jesus wept." Mr. J. scrawled that on the blackboard with a flourish.

So that's common knowledge.

I'm sure, though, that between the pages of the Gospels, Jesus shed a few tears not recorded.

I'm an intrigued fan—a fancier, a buff—of the Bible verses that no one sends home for Vacation Bible School memory badges or to print on a tea towel—a book for another day. Just not meaty enough or as black-and-white as we like. Ambiguity, loose ends, unfinished business, and uncertainty all make us Christian folk squirm a bit.

This is one of those verses: "Jesus did many other things as well. If every one of them were written down, I suppose that even the whole world would not have room for the books that would be written" (John 21:25).

What? There's stuff we don't know?

In my mind, this makes it open season for our imaginations. What else happened? What miracles wound up on the cutting room floor? What Jesus jokes would've been added as postscripts? Would the disciples have appeared more "with it" and less concerned about their hierarchy in the kingdom? Or, with each passing narrative, would they have been more like us, modern and educated and evolved disciples— pettier, more argumentative, more opinionated, more bullish?

Besides Nicodemus, were there unnamed truth-seeking Pharisees who sought Him out in secret alleyways or clandestine campgrounds? Would there have been other sentences that would've made it onto Mr. Jurkowski's "Best of" lists? Maybe—Jesus laughed. Jesus sang. Jesus ran. Jesus bled.

We can only guess. Keeping consistent with Jesus' character, though, and His affinity for the regular, everyday stuff of life that He liked to include in His tender tales, I can envision His eyes moistening at the sight of children skipping hand in hand or his mother dancing at a festive wedding. Or perhaps tears fell at the death of Joseph, the man who, despite public opinion, had the faith to embrace a "virgin-not-a-virgin." Which was it anyway? The good people of Nazareth deserve to know. It remains fascinating to me that, out of respect for Mary and God's plan—and for the set-apart sanctity of the immaculate conception—Jesus' earthly father did not lie with his wife until after the birth of Jesus. Can we give this man a few more props, please?

We have records of three incidents when Jesus cried like us "mere mortals": Lazarus, Jesus pining over Jerusalem as a mother hen gathering her errant chicks, and Gethsemane at the apex of His

> One thing that grief will give you—if you allow it to stay with you long enough to reap its ripened rewards: Compassion. Care. Empathy.

anguish (John 11:35; Luke 19:41; Hebrews 5:7–9). But can't you imagine more?

Why? Because Jesus modeled compassion and care and empathy as the best of humanity. The gold standard. And one thing that grief will give you—if you allow it to stay with you long enough to reap its ripened rewards—is, well, actually those three things. Compassion. Care. Empathy.

Interesting how God chooses the way to dispense them. Or so I reflected on that day.

The profile was unmistakable. As I excused myself past the two people on the end of the row and took my place on the concrete amphitheater seat alongside my son and his wife, I stole a sidelong glance.

Yep. That was her. Sitting directly behind my son.

I felt her eyes on me from the moment I sat down. My neck prickled with the conjured-up image of her gaze, and my cheeks burned, though not from the warm springtime sun heating up the packed theater and now bouncing off the pavement.

How could this have happened? Of all the Easter Services orchestrated throughout Southern California—no doubt, hundreds—I ended up here. In this seat. At this service.

Really, God?

Really?

Pastor Chad was way off on his Easter message too. He was

not preaching, "Hallelujah. They rolled away the stone. Etcetera. Etcetera." He was off on some tangent about loving your enemy. Clearly, Chad had not gotten the memo about the tenor of an Easter service salvation message. I was counting on the Holy Spirit to straighten that one out. Pronto.

No, God. Uh-uh.

And so it started on one particular Easter Sunday.

I think if you live long enough, you'll have a Sunday or two (or fifteen) like that as well. All to remind you that things don't always go as planned.

Maybe that's why *pivot* reigns as the word of the decade.

Luke 4 showcases some fancy footwork on Jesus' part.

Pivot would be putting it mildly.

Having just bested Satan at his own temptation game, and after forty days in the wilderness, we are told that "Jesus returned to Galilee in the power of the Spirit" (v. 14). Not that He wasn't already filled with the Spirit, but apparently He was supercharged at this juncture, as was evidenced by His spellbinding teaching throughout Galilee.

Jesus entered the synagogue of His youth, reading from Isaiah the prophet. Likely in front of those who had watched Him mature, these same Nazarene neighbors now in attendance remained stubbornly stymied by the miraculous stories that rolled into town with Him.

Jesus was clearly trending. And the hometown trolls were waiting to take Him down a notch.

Unrolling the scroll handed to Him—here's where I like to imagine what unrolling an ancient scroll sounded like; *ooh*, gives me goosebumps—Jesus read Isaiah's words.

> The Spirit of the Sovereign Lord is on me,
> because the Lord has anointed me

> to proclaim good news to the poor.
> He has sent me to *bind up the brokenhearted*,
> to proclaim *freedom for the captives*
> and *release from darkness* for the prisoners,
> to proclaim the year of the Lord's favor.
>
> (Isaiah 61:1–2, emphasis added)

I love the next stage note.

Then he rolled up the scroll, gave it back to the attendant and sat down. (Luke 4:20)

Simple. Succinct. Short and sweet.

Never one to miss a moment of impact by letting words hover and hang, Jesus said nothing, took His place sitting (making clear that He would deliver the accompanying sermon), and I like to imagine, read the room.

Did He make eye contact with childhood friends there that day? Perhaps other Nazarene boys who had studied the Torah with Him in His adolescence, remembering now His affection and aptitude for the Scriptures. Did He nod to those who had enlisted His services for repairs or known Joseph for his trade? Stare softly but knowingly at some who had speculated about the timeline of Mary's marriage and Jesus' birth? Perhaps He smiled at neighbors who had joined their caravan when traveling to Jerusalem for the feast of the Passover. Wasn't there that forgotten story about twelve-year-old Jesus getting lost and being found again in the temple, teaching to astonished onlookers?

Were the pieces falling into place or falling into disbelief?

Now this same boy—a man lean and darkened by his days in the wilderness—was standing before them reading with such authority.

"The eyes of everyone in the synagogue were fastened on him" (Luke 4:20).

"Eyes fastened on him" packs a punch bowl full of meaning.

The only thing I've experienced that is in the least bit reminiscent of that moment is ten minutes smack-dab in the middle of Manhattan. In the Broadway play *Death and the Maiden*, three spectacular actors, Gene Hackman, Glenn Close, and Richard Dreyfus, riveted the audience with their compelling lines. However, the most spine-tingling, eye-popping, powerful moments were the silent ones. A rarity in the world of live theater, where dialogue carries the burden of engaging the audience, as opposed to film where silent close-ups carry the day.

The audience watches, transfixed, as Close, in the role of an abuse victim, eavesdrops on a conversation that the perpetrator is having with her husband, and we are drawn into the moment, and specifically to her, without one word being spoken.

That was the make-believe world though—a stunning script, but made up, shaded by moody lighting, exacting set design, painstaking blocking, and three award-winning thespians moving inch by inch as directed under the magical lights of Broadway. With years of experience, professional expertise, and the sleight of hand intrinsic in theater, those ten minutes unfolded exactly as planned. Orchestrated to a tee. Executed to perfection after hundreds of rehearsals and performances.

But this was Jesus.

Solo. Unplugged. Pared down, yet maxed out in His minimalism.

The God-Man, alone with the scroll inked with the words that described Him.

I'm sure the magnetism flowing from those moments remains incomparable to any other earthly situation. My example is a weak analogy left wanting, not meant to be a comparison, only to prove what power can be capsulized in silence. That is what I imagined those moments to be like—the longer-than-measured minutes between Jesus handing the scroll back to the attendant and taking His place in the quieted crowd.

The silent audience, with all eyes fastened on Him. Hushed. Expectant. Spellbound. Could've-heard-a-pin-drop.

Then, the bombshells began. Jesus launched them from His seat. Shock and awe set in.

"Today this scripture is fulfilled in your hearing" (v. 21).

"Isn't this Joseph's son?" (v. 22). The murmurs snapped in the space like electricity, heating a swirling undertow within the anger building. Surely Joseph's son couldn't really be saying that He is the one spoken about by the prophet?

Somehow Jesus knew they were expecting a pretty big miracle to back up those claims.

Never one to shy away from controversy, Jesus didn't let up, but threw fuel onto the fire. He suggested that they were the ones with a fickle faith, not accepting Him as other towns had. He infuriated them by suggesting that Gentiles would be embraced by God and that some of them—the chosen people, the ones in the synagogue this very day—would not be considered Yahweh's celestial shoo-ins.

Jesus spoke of a God who bestows favor upon ones seemingly so underrated and undeserving. Those on the outside of this in-crowd. Those whom circumstance has thrown to the outside, into a spinning world of disbelief and grief, with their faces—ahem, your face—pressed to the glass, peering in.

Jesus forever championing the underdog.

Such a bad look for a messiah.

The crowd's response: "All the people in the synagogue were furious when they heard this. They got up, drove him out of the town, and took him to the brow of the hill on which the town was built, in order to throw him off the cliff. But he walked right through the crowd and went on his way" (vv. 28–30).

The mob had spoken.

Luke didn't explain how Jesus escaped, just that He did. Perhaps that pivot is the miracle the crowd asked for but failed to see.

That story reminds me of what often happens to us. We start the day with one idea about how life will go and then respond in a new way by changing direction, after it's clear that the day is not going to go as planned.

Pivoting plus.

On that Easter Sunday while I sat in a California amphitheater, it was clear that I was going to need a push to pivot with poise.

I had prayed for God to transform my grief to something He could use. I was dutifully collecting my losses in the recycling bin and kept peeking in to see if they were still there. I figured that one day I would find an empty bin and then announce, "Okay, world. I'm back. Signed. Sealed. Delivered. I'm Yours"—accentuated on the downbeat, thanks to Stevie Wonder.

Sort of a passive pivot. Like changes in the heart that I knew about privately, not ones that I would have to display in a way that called me to leave my bubble bath, my besties, and my Bible.

Yet here I was, without two of those three. And Pastor Chad droning on and on about blessing our enemies. Everything in the amphitheater blurred, like the f-stop had been altered in my eyeballs, changing the depth of field, and all was out of focus. Chad's words remained the only stimuli allowed in by my senses.

The conflict accelerated.

No, God. You've got the wrong girl. I'm still smarting, Lord.

"I have come to bind up the wounds of the brokenhearted."

Wait. Was that coming through the PA?

It reminded me of a random news story that had stuck with me for, I dunno, twenty years? The bawdy entertainer-comedian Sam Kinison, steeped in a childhood of faith, fleetingly survived a head-on highway collision en route to a gig in the Las Vegas area. Witnesses say he spoke some words immediately following the accident and began having a conversation with, well, no one. It sounded as if he were arguing with somebody, looking upward and saying something about not being ready or not wanting to go, ending the audibly one-sided discussion with an acquiescent, "Oh. Okay."

Then he died. On the spot. A weak "okay" on his lips.

Whether that had happened exactly as reported, I'll never know. What I do know is that the account had hung around my memory bank, and I suddenly felt like the person having the debate with an invisible someone was me.

Don't get me wrong. I had written in one of my "journals"—pink Post-it collages in an old design-school notebook—the following: "We need to seek transcendent values that make the temporal bearable for us and for others." Then I had listed those very values that I would set my sights on: kindness, patience, insight, recognition of unresolved pain behind words, and behaviors, and—as icing on the cake, the granddaddy of all—forgiveness. With an exclamation point, no less.

To this summary I added, "These will be cultivated by us in our struggle and harvested in our pain."

Oh, so lofty my words. So poetic. You just stay in that notebook, words. Where you belong.

On the top of the page, I had printed in a bold orange marker, "Continuing Education: Learning from my Losses."

Continuing education was not a new concept to me. Trained as a dental hygienist, I regularly needed to keep educating myself about improved methodologies or current scientific studies to preserve my state licensing. Not unlike twelve-step programs, which suggest regular meetings and accountability, all professional designations require continuing education.

Maintaining a life that keeps us free from the ravages of grief begs for ongoing care as well.

One of the nuggets I learned in Divorce Recovery—part of my

continuing education—was an answer to the question that everyone in that cohort asks repeatedly: "What do I do next?"

I love the crisp answer: "The next right thing."

Well, I loved it, that is, when I was safely ensconced in the small group at church that taught me that.

I hated that it came to mind on that Sunday.

The "next right thing" is contained in Matthew 6:33: "But seek first his kingdom and his righteousness, and all these things will be given to you as well." Rather than laboring over the specifics of individual tough decisions, I knew it was better to labor over the condition of my heart so that the right decisions would flow from that, on an as-needed basis.

That's why, under continuing education, I had another list, one of the spiritual disciplines—items I considered the stepping stones to "seek first His kingdom." It could have also been titled "The Next Right Things." To maintain the heart posture that would ensure freedom from bitterness, I knew the spiritual work had to be ongoing so that the new story would continue to be written with God's hand.

You can find various listings of spiritual disciplines and use various words to describe them. I knew instinctively, though, that spiritual discipline meant exercising my spiritual self just as regularly as my physical self, which had become second nature to me the more I did it. It was a habit of the heart, protecting me from a future framed by regret or shame or sorrow.

Spiritual discipline was embodied in community—for me, small groups and Bible studies—where I could share the disciplines of *prayer* and *Scripture study* and *service*. It was inherent with my friends and family and times around the table of *celebration* and the joy those times would release, including celebrating small victories I accomplished along the way of my healing. Practices of *simplicity* and *solitude*, *meditation* and *self-reflection*, translated to a freshly evaluated lifestyle developed via alone time that challenged me to identify what I was clinging to for meaning and identity.

Alone time under jacaranda trees, walking through purple rain.

I intended to put all those things into practice. At a premeditated and perfect time.

For me.

Yet here I sat, on a warm April morning, with more than the sun flushing my face.

"I have come to bind up the brokenhearted."

I had to imaginatively insert myself into that first-century temple in Nazareth that day when Isaiah's words were read, though I would have been hearing them while hiding behind the pillars on the porch with the other nontraditional, rather naughty "Marys"—girls who weren't supposed to be listening. Would His eyes have found mine, searching for me around that pillar as if to nudge me to higher thinking, to a heavenly agenda, one that could not be contained by the limitations of the earth's orbit (or the cultural expectations of the day)?

Or would I have run breathlessly behind the crowd toward the brow of the hill, granting tacit support?

The silent debate raged, and then I found myself acquiescing, with a weak *okay* on my lips followed by my less-than-angelic conditional caveat, "Okay, if I turn around and open my mouth, You'd better supply the words. 'Cause I got nothin', Lord."

I don't remember the rest of the sermon.

I just remember that it ended. And when it did, I spun and faced the proverbial "other woman," certainly not the woman who had inflicted the greatest harm to my marriage, but a woman whose presence had been the source of anguish and heartache for me—and by extension, for my children. She stood staring at me, wide-eyed, with a look that said she had no idea what this confrontation would hold. Little did she know that I didn't either.

I took a deep breath.

I opened my mouth, wondering what in the world was going to come out. At the same time, my arms automatically extended, and I drew her close to me so that I could speak into her ear without anyone hearing. I considered it the ultimate confidential conversation between the three of us—her, me, and that invisible Someone who had been prodding my heart in the most persistent of ways. In all fairness, she didn't pull away. Perhaps that invisible Someone had spoken to her, too, at the same time.

Honestly, I don't remember my exact words. But I am certain of their intent. It went something like this, "I know you have been hurt, and I pray that God will bind up your wounds and heal your heart. I forgive you, and I pray for God's blessings over you today."

I felt like I was channeling Chad, using words like "bind up." I was asking myself, *Who says that?* as they were coming out of my mouth. Uh. Hellloooo. I think that's the Holy Spirit, girl.

As I let go and turned to walk away, I stopped dead in my tracks. The sound of what I could only describe as chains falling away deafened me. My eyes frantically searched the amphitheater to see if others were hearing it too. In fact, initially, I was *sure* that everyone was hearing it. I believed that huge, eighteen-wheeler-size metal rings were hitting the concrete and shaking the stage with the soundwaves, but no one seemed to notice. I was the only one searching for the source of the sounds. Clearly, I was the only one hearing them.

"I have come to set the captives free."

As in "breaking my chains," Lord?

I guess I didn't choose the brow of the hill.

Henri Nouwen wrote,

Compassion asks us to go where it hurts to enter into the places of pain, to share in brokenness, fear, confusion, and anguish.

Compassion challenges us to cry out with those in misery, to mourn with those who are lonely, to weep with those in tears. Compassion requires us to be weak with the weak, vulnerable with the vulnerable, and powerless with the powerless. Compassion means immersion in the condition of being human.[1]

Well, Henri, you were right. That hurt.

Here's what I believe with my whole heart, though. God will lead people to us who need forgiveness, a new identity, or a word of hope from the pages of our stories. We should expect miraculous meetings to take place before our healing is complete, as helping others is part of the healing process. It's faith meeting vulnerability—all in God's timing, not ours.

> God will lead people to us who need forgiveness, a new identity, or a word of hope from the pages of our stories.

To be clear, I don't believe that forgiving someone necessitates initiating or maintaining a relationship with that someone. Or that face-to-face meetings are essential to effective or genuine forgiveness. I'm a big believer in boundaries to protect one's emotional health. Emotional health is paramount to the Jesus of the Gospels.

But I couldn't deny the extraordinary circumstances that led me to one particular spot in one particular moment with one particular person who came bearing the unmistakable *imago Dei*. I wasn't brave. I wasn't thrilled with the prospect. I wasn't a spiritual superhero. I simply did not want to pass up the possibility that God could do the spectacular by my just stepping out of His way. I suspected He knew that I could handle this, and I trusted the result was in His hands.

I was more afraid of missing His work in my life than I was of making a fool of myself.

I was more afraid that my pain would be wasted. I just could not live with that thought.

> The Spirit of the Sovereign LORD is on me,
> because the LORD has anointed me
> to proclaim good news to the poor.
> He has sent me to *bind up the brokenhearted*,
> to *proclaim freedom for the captives*
> and release from darkness for the prisoners,
> to proclaim the year of the LORD's favor.
>
> (ISAIAH 61:1–2, EMPHASIS ADDED)

Compassion. Care. Empathy. The gold standard.

Starting the day with one idea about how it will go, and responding in a new way by changing direction, after it's clear that it won't go as planned.

Yeah. I'll still go with *pivot* being the word of the decade.

Seeing life differently after trauma is a choice. Start with choosing the path to wellness. And then commit to continuing education that grooms the path. And the reward for that act of the will—that choice, that step of faith, that step into the unknown abyss—is the sound of chains falling away.

Binding up the brokenhearted. Freeing the captive. At one and the same time.

Crazy Spinach Salad

So pretty on an Easter buffet table. The strawberries are often at their early peak in their season, and the mix of the buttery avocado is a marriage made in heaven.

I include two recipes in this chapter because this duo just pairs together so beautifully. I always make them for the same meal.

DRESSING

1/4 cup apple cider vinegar

1/2 cup canola oil

2 tablespoons sesame seeds

1 tablespoon poppy seeds

1/2 cup sugar

1 1/2 tablespoons minced onion

1/2 teaspoon salt

1/2 teaspoon Worcestershire sauce

1/2 teaspoon paprika

1/2 teaspoon chopped fresh mint

SALAD

2 (8-ounce) bags spinach leaves, washed

10 to 12 ounces strawberries, sliced

2 to 4 medium to large avocados, sliced

DIRECTIONS

1. In a medium bowl whisk together the vinegar, oil, sesame and poppy seeds, sugar, onion, salt, Worcestershire sauce, paprika, and mint,

or put the ingredients in a large glass jar and shake. Refrigerate until ready to use.

2. In a large salad bowl, just before serving, combine the spinach, strawberries, and avocados. Toss. Add the dressing lightly and toss to combine. Taste and add more dressing as per personal preference. Makes 8 servings.

Mushroom Crust Quiche

A perfect pairing with the tangy and sweet Crazy Spinach Salad. I serve them side by side at Eastertime.

I first made this quiche when I was a new cook, and it's remained a favorite and flavorful twist on the regular quiche Lorraine. I've made it for so long I'm not sure where the dog-eared recipe card originated, but quiche is one of those dishes you can easily make your own. Try substituting crumbled sausage for the ham, spinach for the parsley, or caramelized onions for the green onions.

INGREDIENTS

½ cup (1 stick) butter, divided

¾ pound baby bella mushrooms, coarsely chopped

1 cup crushed saltine crackers

¾ cup chopped green onions

3 cups shredded jack cheese, divided

1 cup full-fat cottage cheese

3 eggs

¼ teaspoon cayenne pepper

4 ounces minced ham (mince by hand or in a food processor)

¼ cup chopped Italian parsley

DIRECTIONS

1. Preheat the oven to 350 degrees. Grease a 9-inch pie pan.
2. Melt 6 tablespoons of the butter in a medium to large sauté pan over medium heat. Add the mushrooms and cook until soft. Stir in the crushed crackers. Spoon the mixture into the pie pan and pat to cover the bottom and halfway up the sides.

3. Wipe out the sauté pan and then melt the remaining 2 tablespoons of butter. Add the onions and cook until tender. Sprinkle the onions onto the crust, followed by 2 cups of the cheese. You can cover with plastic wrap and finish the next day at this point.

4. To proceed, in a blender or mixer, whirl the cottage cheese, eggs, and cayenne until smooth. Pour into the crust and sprinkle with paprika.

5. Bake 20 to 25 minutes until set and not wobbly in the center.

6. After removing from the oven and while still warm, top with the minced ham, the remaining 1 cup cheese, and the parsley.

7. Serve warmish or at room temperature.

Makes 8 servings.

CHAPTER 13

THE NIGHTMARE ENDS

As he went along, he saw a man blind from birth.
His disciples asked him, "Rabbi, who sinned,
this man or his parents, that he was born blind?"

"Neither this man nor his parents sinned," said Jesus, "but this
happened so that the works of God might be displayed in him."
—JOHN 9:1–3

MY SWEDISH GRANDMOTHER, MONNIE—KNOWN TO THE READER as the thoroughly-modern-former-Hilma-now-Thelma from chapter 6—had a way with words, veiled hats, and the color purple. As an impressionable little girl, I loved the rich and royal violet hues and the millinery magic, but I cherished her words most of all.

She helped me memorize the books of the Bible, cheering me on from the blue brocade couch in the "fancy" living room while I recited the titles and rolled around on the carpet with the cats, the way most eight-year-olds tackled the problem of short attention span and decimated any kind of "fancy" in one fell swoop.

Monnie, swathed in her purple silk scarf, applauded enthusiastically even when I got the First and Second Samuel and First and

Second Kings sections a little out of order. Deuteronomy loomed as the big hurdle, and she seemed to understand that anything after that was just gravy. And gravy was a big deal back then, believe me.

The words I really waited to hear, though, were the ones she whispered to me in the kitchen nook right inside the sliding pocket door that squealed when she closed it behind us, the coveted space where our one phone with the cartoonishly stretched-out cord hung on the wall. That's where she'd take a crisp five-dollar bill out of her pocket—I think equal to about $300 today—slip it into my palm, and confess clandestinely, "You're my favorite."

I don't know how many crisp five-dollar bills she kept in those pockets, but I'm sure she managed to cut each of us kids out of the herd for that little conversation on a regular basis. I suppose she knew that we would eventually believe it.

Sneaky grandma.

What if you were constantly told how favored you were? What if it didn't matter if Kings and Samuel got transposed or if you remembered Deuteronomy at all? Or if your short attention span had you veering off course sometimes with only your cat as company, and it didn't matter? What if you were given gifts that were yours and yours alone? What if you only remembered squeaky doors with a smile because you remembered the prize—the good stuff—that came next?

Next. That's what this chapter's about. I hope that you're feeling more ready for that word.

Next. What's waiting for you and who's waiting to call you out as special, smart, set apart, and celebrated all at the same time—like Monnie did for me when I was a child, and like Jesus' words did for me when I was a "growed-up girl" sporting a bruised heart and skinned knees.

Next. The space where you leave the angst of grief in the dust and view your world with new frames, new glasses, new insight, and an expectation of redeemed purposes.

Next. Where you discard the names that labeled you worthless and instead wear monikers like *Beloved* monogrammed on your heart and tattooed on your palm to read every time you stretch your arms to the sky first thing in the morning.

Next. Where you abandon unhealthy distractions and enlist proper ones to fill space and time with peace and purpose.

Next. Where compassion and caring reflect God's image in your life and bitterness is kept at bay with spiritual disciplines standing as sentries to your soul.

Next. Where squishy hearts are ones not crushed with the weight of grief, but softened by the tears of others.

Next. Where forgiveness can live alongside healthy boundaries and a community of Jesus followers and wise professionals helping you clarify and define both.

Next. Where you celebrate small victories and draw confidence from how far you've come, and when you string those two things together, they turn upward, indicating a healing trajectory.

Next. Where the memory of the grief clearly remains, as it always will, but it's remembered differently now, with the pain distinctively tempered.

Next. Anticipated. Forward-looking. Hope-filled. Futuristic.

If you were at Disneyland, I'd be walking you toward Tomorrowland.

No more Fantasyland for you. And Adventureland's a given.

Not that there won't be setbacks. Or missteps. Or, "Please, can I begin again?" Heck, I had to throw out a whole batch of cookie dough while I was recipe testing the other day, because it was just, well, awful.

I invoke a twenty-four-hour rule when unplanned hiccups happen.

I allow myself to sink deeply into a beanbag chair without washing my face for twenty-four hours and then, out with the lipstick and

I invoke a twenty-four-hour rule when unplanned hiccups happen.

chilled silicone eye patches and skinny jeans or mom high-rises, depending upon your preference—just something other than those tired, grieving-gray sweats.

I get outside and take a long walk—straight-shooter-lament-type convos with God in tow—and connect with a friend and have Alexa serenade me with worship songs while I chop onions for minestrone and open tin cans with abandon for my college roommate's famous dump cake (to be enjoyed later with vanilla ice cream and a pot of Earl Grey for my fifth screening of *Downton Abbey*).

I page through my binder of encouraging scripture taken from my "wailing wall." I meet up with that "hooligan with a handsaw" who makes me laugh until I cry. I drive to the inspiring nursery at the top of the hill and meander through all the flowers and heirloom tomato seedlings and stop at my favorite French bakery that makes cinnamon vanilla steamer foam art in the shape of palm fronds. I take a deep breath and sit quietly in the sunshine.

I recognize the direction I'm headed and then interrupt the binding, electricity-like current keeping me hostage. I flip the breaker switch.

I've got my list of go-tos and hopefully, now, you've got yours too.

I take responsibility for recalibrating my life so that the inside matches the outside, except in this case, it's the stuff we do on the outside that nudges the inside to a healthy response and the recognition that something's gotta give.

Those down days will come. And it's okay. It's just not okay for those to be the norm anymore.

I hope you've seen that Jesus' presence upends norms. He overturns society's hierarchy of values at every turn, most notably in how women adopt permanently broken valuations of themselves in the shadow of significant loss. Jesus tangles with those perceptions as intentionally as He did with His temple table-tipping.

And He can upend the cluttered and dirty tables in your life that you assumed were bolted to the floor.

As we draw closer to God's intended image for us, we can expect doubts and second-guessing to crop up. That's when we enlist the strategies starting with the I AM who claims you as His reflection. Your "Royal I AM-ish-ness."

One thing's for certain, though. With a mustard seed of faith and a consistent personal "working out of our grief"—shades of Paul's "working out our salvation" (Philippians 2:12)—there will come a time when the nightmare ends.

Once upon a time, not so very long ago—or back in chapter 1—I had written about the nightmare living in my closet, typing, "It returned every night like clockwork, stalking my sleep. Within its angry visits, a phantom voice sobbed, 'I can't find me anywhere,' and not recognizing that as my own cry, I remember thinking, *That poor, poor girl. She can't find herself anywhere.*"

Except, unlike fairy tales that also begin with *Once upon a time*, this was a reality in my life. I couldn't find myself anywhere.

I had grown used to this replay but never to the despair that rode in tandem with it. I wondered if it would ever stop. I had hoped that it would just go away respectfully. I wasn't looking for a movie-matinee resolution.

Jesus had other plans, though. Like He did in the healing of the blind man recorded in John 9.

Walking down the street, Jesus saw a man blind from birth. His disciples asked, "Rabbi, who sinned: this man or his parents, caus-ing him to be born blind?" Jesus said, "You're asking the wrong question. You're looking for someone to blame. There is no such cause-effect here. Look instead for what God can do." . . . He said this and then spit in the dust, made a clay paste with the saliva, rubbed the paste on the blind man's eyes, and said, "Go, wash at the Pool of Siloam" (Siloam means "Sent"). The man went and washed—and saw. (John 9:1–7 MSG)

From my earliest memory, this story fascinated yet confounded me. It remained such a mystery that Jesus spit into His hands. What's up with that? As a kid, every parent's voice echoed with "Wash your hands" and "No spitting," mostly to all the boys (except on the baseball diamond where, naturally, it was given a pass). Now, Jesus was doing exactly what we were told not to do. I was confused. Was it magic saliva? Magic dirt? Or both?

What did Jesus' followers think as they watched him do this? What was going through their minds? What was the point? After all, the show was for their benefit. More specifically, how did the doubting Pharisees interpret His actions that seem so bizarre to us in the pandemic's postapocalyptic, germophobic age?

It turns out, dust of the ground, spittle, and clay from which man was molded, all point to creation and the divine One who claimed to wield it. The oral traditions and extrabiblical texts underscored this thinking as a firmly held belief among those who were watching.

This is what the Jews of Jesus' era acknowledged. That humans were made up of those three things: Saliva. Molded clay. Dust. All the ingredients that Jesus packed on the blind man's eyes. Not a random recipe.

I hardly believe He needed any tricks to heal the man blind from birth. No sleight of hand to distract. But Jesus was the master of multiple meanings, constantly challenging His audience with His symbolism and reference to Jewish and cultural ideologies. He would know that the witnesses to this miracle would interpret these three things—dust, saliva, clay—as referencing the genesis of humanity.

Perhaps Jesus, in mixing up this holy hunk of mud, was continuing to boldly and publicly pronounce Himself Creator, at one with the Father. The divine I AM with no beginning and no end from which all life—and all sight—was spawned.

I reflected on that as I spit into the tube that would go off to the genetic tracing labs of the ancestry company. Contained within my own saliva were the twisted-ladder, identity-laden strands that made me, me. I know that because Mr. Close, in Honors Biology class, showed us the distinctive DNA diagrams back in tenth grade. But I marveled that the ancient world somehow understood that, too, without Mr. Close or the magical electron microscope's pictures showing the beauty of our genetic packaging. Human saliva contains remarkable components of humankind, the orderly yet unique patterns representing life at its inception, the very building blocks of who we are.

These were the same double helix strands that I was sure had been unwound, unfurled, stripped clean, and found flapping in the wind, doctored and altered by the trauma of my losses. Turns out, that's not too far off. Scientific studies and insightful neurological imaging have shown that trauma has the potential to change future generations because it changes our brains, and the resultant expressions of our genes.[1] In short, there most likely is a pre-trauma and post-trauma "me," and likewise, a pre- and post- "you." At the very tiniest microscopic levels, we are not the same people.

So it made sense that one night, many months after the first nightmare crawled out of my closet and onto my bed, there was a slight but powerful amendment to my dream. It happened just once, and has never happened again. It never needed to.

It started the same way, with my face disappearing into glistening sand, like crystals running through an hourglass, only onto a pile on the floor. A beautiful and noble angel scoops it up, cups the crystals in her hands, and bringing them to her lips, blows the sand (aka me) into the air. Only this time Jesus enters, crouches down to collect those same grains in the palm of His hand, spits into them, and mixes the dust into a paste. Molding clay with His fingers—pressing and turning with intention, the same pressing and turning with which He begins to form my features onto the faceless apparition hovering nearby, somehow watching while at the same time sensing the pressure as He touches and forms a new face. I am being reshaped, recreated, and resurrected amid the dunes of what I had incorrectly assumed to be random and forgotten, unclaimed, and unnamed specks of sand.

> I am being reshaped, recreated, and resurrected amid the dunes of what I had incorrectly assumed to be random and forgotten, unclaimed, and unnamed specks of sand.

Dust of the ground. Saliva. Molded clay. A picture of creation with divine DNA. Doctored. Changed. Forever altered. Formed from the dust of the ground and the spit from His lips.

"He put mud on my eyes," the man replied, "and I washed, and now I see" (John 9:15).

Another voice joined in, "He put mud on my face," and I, for the first time, recognized that as my own cry. After He placed the clay, after He sculpted my new face, He led me to the Pool of Siloam as well. To that pool meaning "sent." To the waters rippling with the whispered promise of that one word.

Sent me to a writing workshop that I had never intended to join, and without which I would never have penned a word. Sent me to a successful yet humble author who, like me, was looking to redeem her pain. Sent me to a smart, resourceful agent and a bright light of a writing coach, who believed that Jesus could repurpose discarded things—and people. Sent me to an experienced editor who I knew would offer me a master class in creative writing and critical thinking.

Sent me to a hot amphitheater on a bright Easter Sunday so that I could hear the unmistakable echo of my chains of unforgiveness fall away. Sent me to a concrete bench outside of a medical building where a silent stranger had been likewise sent to comfort me. Sent me to an irreverent acting class in the heart of Hollywood with a bagful of snickerdoodles and broken dreams.

Maybe He sent me to you. Covered in streaks of mud after washing at the place called Sent.

And like Jacob Marley's three ghosts in Charles Dickens's timeless *A Christmas Carol*, maybe you could see your past, present, and future redeemed, reframed, and restored all because He took my dirt, my pain, my despair, and gathered it all together, spit into it, and mixed and molded a new beginning.

A visit to the past, to understand from what person, place, and position you derived your identity.

A look at the present, to recognize that you are not invisible despite what any nightmare or date on your birth certificate tells you.

A glimpse of the future, to a new life that can exist without that other part of you that is now gone.

Jesus answered them, "You're looking for someone to blame. There is no such cause-effect here. Look instead for what God can do" (John 9:3–5 MSG).

Time to fill those stretched-out, formerly grief-filled places in your heart with joy. To look to see what God can do.

Joy of new possibilities. Joy of new beginnings. Fresh starts.
Joy of new relationships. Joy of deepened community. Joy of simmering spaghetti sauce on the stovetop and chocolate cake dotted with candles to celebrate.

Joy of crunchy fall leaves underfoot and streaky cirrus clouds
    overhead and stark sticks of cherry trees blossoming in
    pink puffs in between.
Joy of old meaning better. Wiser. Tarnish giving way to patina.
Joy of serving.
Joy of intimacy when you're given the honor to share in others'
    griefs.
Joy of forgiveness freeing you.

You are valued. You are esteemed. You are seen. You are named.
You are renewed. You are restored. You are . . .
    Daughter.
Born of dust of the earth, spittle, and molded clay.

Dump Cake

It's so emotionally satisfying to "dump" all these ingredients into a pan without having to measure a thing. My roommate and I made this in college (I thought we were geniuses). And humble, too, especially because I couldn't cook a lick unless it involved chocolate chips. This warm, fruity "cake" served with a scoop of vanilla ice cream doubled both my culinary repertoire and my love of cobbler-type desserts.

This recipe, and iterations of it, has been around so long it's kinda like classical music that belongs to the public domain. Spread your wings and try other substitutions in the pie-filling category.

INGREDIENTS

1 (21-ounce) can cherry pie filling

1 (20-ounce) can crushed pineapple with juice

1 (15-ounce) box yellow cake mix

1 cup (2 sticks) butter, melted

1 cup chopped walnuts or slivered almonds

1 cup sweetened shredded coconut

DIRECTIONS

1. Preheat the oven to 325 degrees.
2. Layer the cherry pie filling and the pineapple in an ungreased 9 x 11-inch baking pan. Sprinkle the cake mix over the fruit and follow with the melted butter, nuts, and coconut.
3. Bake for 1 hour.

Makes 24 servings.

CLOSING THOUGHTS

*She remembered, too, how in her first days . . . when things
had looked so bleak, so terrifying, so tragic . . . it was at
those moments that God's grace came, and that God's
plan was revealed, though it was revealed in His time.
"I can't see it, Lord, but I know You can," she said.*
—ABRAHAM VERGHESE

THE END.

So much contained in those two short words.

This end marks a new beginning for me—and for you.

I never thought I would be writing a book at the same time I qualified for Social Security. I never thought anyone would pay a dime for anything I had to say. I never thought a woman with a senior discount would be taken seriously at any place other than the Michael's checkout register.

Despite the fact that women started to be taken seriously on a professional level when I was a student at UCLA and that my own family reflected this, with three successful sisters—devoted moms all: a sister who is an MD, a second sister who owns her own business, and a third who wears the title of Global VP. Despite all that, and the fact I had known Jesus intimately *forever*, I thought my divorce, financial decline, and struggles with mental and physical health threw me into a lump with all the other has-beens.

I avoided high school reunions. In twelfth grade, I was voted Most Likely to Succeed, and I felt like if I did show up, the disappointed alumni would be calling for a recount, for me to turn in my title. Or at least for an announcement to apologize for the error. I was not "most" of anything, let alone successful.

All those negative beliefs because I had measured my worth with all that could, and did, disappear in a startlingly short period of time.

That's where this end comes in. It walked offstage with the first chapter and emerged as something else by chapter 13.

And for you, my new friend, if I have helped you discover your true worth and identity, buried in the bosom of God, then I can die with a smile on my lips—preferably amid the grove of leafy spring-green trees on my favorite walk, with my AARP card tucked securely inside my right shoe.

Your pain is my why, your pain is my reason, your pain is the burden that I want to carry with you.

I am so honored to do so.

Let's not have this be our end. But our beginning. For the both of us.

ACKNOWLEDGMENTS

WHEN YOU WRITE YOUR FIRST BOOK AT SIXTY-EIGHT YEARS OF AGE, you invariably want to thank everyone in your whole life for everything. Partly because you think that the sand is running through the hourglass so quickly that you'll never get to write another book acknowledgment again and partly because you're bubbling over with the joy this project has brought. It just feels right to share it with, well, everyone in the whole wide world.

So as not to disappoint, I will acknowledge that I enjoyed a charmed childhood, and for that I have my parents to thank. I had a smart, reading mother who taught me about planting pansies and canning summer's peaches and a father whom I admired for his intelligence and work ethic. I had a grandmother who slipped me five-dollar bills and told me I was her favorite (she did that with all my siblings) and a grandfather who cooked and made amazing cinnamony applesauce and brought us chocolate bars. In that environment I never doubted I could succeed or be loved or be anything other than safe. How I wish that every child could feel those things.

Along with the trauma of my I-didn't-see-it-coming separation came three couples whom I still call My Three Angels. My sister and brother-in-law, Linda and Dave Roark; my lifelong pals Mike and Karen Mizrahi; and my high school youth pastors and friends, Ken and Carolyn Kemp. When my predictable life walked out, they walked in. They're still here. Without them, I wonder if *I* would be.

My three college pals (FFs)—Kay, Debra, and Patti—kept setting me upright and winding me back up. Their support in this journey defines friendship. It's hilarious to see them comment on my Instagram posts, because they are so subjectively over-the-top in their accolades.

Chris and Susan Babbitt helped me in countless ways. They have been like gravity in my life: never failing, always reliably present. Just like my baby sister, Laurie, who kept telling me that the branches in the trees were going to bloom again someday. I heard her words as I wrote.

This book's dedication speaks to the admiration I hold for my three adult children: Taylor, Kendall, and KC. All pushed me to stretch myself in new ways. My respect for them only grew in leaps and bounds when they chose such wonderful humans as their partners: Amanda, Tommy, and Bryony. The fact that they gifted me with nine littles is the icing on the cake as far as life goes. The joy of those nine—Hayden, Jett, Judah, Hadley, Cruz, Tig, Scout, Shiloh, and Sherlock—have imparted feelings otherworldly to me. Beyond my capability to articulate.

As for the nitty gritty of the book writing itself, I have to start with my agent, Meredith Brock, and my mentor, Lysa TerKeurst. They own the brainchild that was *The Book Proposal Bootcamp*, the writer's course that started it all. With my daughter Kendall's insistence, I entered the competition wary of my skills and sure I was the token "old lady outlier" they needed to round out the group demographic.

I credit Meredith with the topic of my writing as she suggested for us to "write what you google at three a.m." I did just that.

Lysa remains a bright star in the nonfiction genre, encouraging others to tell their stories, not to scintillate but to instruct. She taught us to reveal our pain, not to wallow in it, so that the reader might believe that we understand theirs. She taught me to hold others' fragility thoughtfully while writing.

The warmth and good humor of my writing coach and facilitator of the boot camp, Amanda Bacon, lifted our entire cohort. Amanda, I'm happy to be your virtual next-door neighbor anytime.

HarperCollins was like the Ringling Brothers' Christmas Circus Train that used to chug by my little cottage on December nights. Awash in color and wonder and all kinds and stripes of characters—in the best possible way. I ached with anticipation while waiting for those railroad cars to pass, and it's the same way I felt about meeting my team at HarperCollins.

Janene MacIvor was the first person I spoke to at HarperCollins. My substantive editor, obviously smart and experienced, was so eager to learn about me.

Not my book. Not my words. But me.

I mean, eventually we had to talk about words, but in the beginning she made me feel like the person behind the words was her special interest. The fact that she was a grandmother, too, created a bond that I hope will last a lifetime. She gently excised with the sweetest disposition and inferred and red-lined without wagging her finger once. How she does it, I'll never know.

Kathryn Notestine (Kathryn with a *y*) also wore an editor's hat. Wise beyond her years, she possessed the gift of zeroing in on something—like a tense that wasn't working—as if she were wearing night-vision goggles in a darkened room. And so darn nice.

Jennifer McNeil rounded out the editorial bench. I drove her crazy with my metaphors and adjectives, but she good-naturedly allowed some while cutting others. I made her promise that if I landed in Belgium, she would let me treat her to some famous chocolate over a coffee, where we could laugh about how many words it took for me to describe something.

All three were like my personal Mensa crew. Like Christmas, right?

The marketing team—Erica Smith, Mark Glesne, and Briá Woods—were super cool "kids" who were especially good at listening. Erica possessed a twinkle in her eye, which spoke to her adventurous spirit; Mark presented solid and logical (and fit) and weighed in on awkward questions with confidence; and Briá responded almost instantaneously to any question I ever had. All pros, all the time.

Lucky me. Even with this messy story, they all helped me sort it out and put it onto the page. How much purpose you have given me. How much fun this has been. I wish it would never end.

To my Lord and Father of the heavenly lights, how is it that the One who hung the stars in the sky cares about me and my words? It is a wonder beyond wonders and will forever cause me to kneel before Your throne. You alone are worthy. Thank you for loving me.

NOTES

Introduction
1. Bonnie Lewis, "300: This Is Voxology," June 14, 2021, in *Voxology*, produced by Tim Stafford and Mike Erre, podcast, MP3 audio, 2:00:00, https://voxologypodcast.com/podcasts/this-is-voxology/.

Chapter 2: Getting to the Root of the Problem
1. "Rebuilding Your Life out of the Rubble with Amy Downs," June 8, 2021, in *For the Love*, produced by Jen Hatmaker, podcast, MP3 audio, 51:21, https://jenhatmaker.com/podcast/series-35/rebuilding-your-life-out-of-the-rubble-with-amy-downs/.

Chapter 4: Stand in Your Pain
1. C. S. Lewis, *The Four Loves* (London: Harcourt Brace & Company, 1960), 78.
2. Henri J. M. Nouwen, *You Are the Beloved: Daily Meditations for Spiritual Living* (New York: Convergent Books, 2017), s.v. "March 18," quoted in "Dare to Stand in Your Suffering," Henri Nouwen Society, March 18, 2022, https://henrinouwen.org/meditations/dare-to-stand-in-your-suffering/.
3. Bill Gaither, *The Jesus Music: The Soundtrack of a Movement*, directed by Jon Erwin and Andrew Erwin (Vancouver: Lionsgate, 2021), https://www.lionsgate.com/movies/the-jesus-music.

Chapter 5: Find Some Friends with Stretchers
1. Tiffany Aliche, "Owning and Knowing Your Finances with the 'Budgetnista,'" July 20, 2021, in *For the Love*, produced by Jen Hatmaker,

225

podcast, MP3 audio, 1:05:25, https://jenhatmaker.com/podcast/series-35
/owning-and-knowing-your-finances-with-the-budgetnista-tiffany-aliche/.

Chapter 6: Who You Say I Am

1. *Roots*, part 1, written by Alex Haley and William Blinn, directed by David
   Greene, aired January 23, 1977, 1:37:00, https://www.imdb.com/title
   /tt1250564/.
2. "Golden Buzzer: Nightbirde's Original Song Makes Simon Cowell
   Emotional—*America's Got Talent* 2021," *America's Got Talent*, June 9, 2021,
   YouTube video, 1:23, https://www.youtube.com/watch?v=CZJvBfoHDk0.

Chapter 7: Seek a Safe Harbor

1. Helen Keller, *The Story of My Life* (1905; repr., New York: Penguin Group,
   2010), 14.
2. Keller, *Story of My Life*, 14.
3. For more information on New Life Ministries, visit NewLife.com or call
   1–800-NEWLIFE.

Chapter 8: New Frames, New Glasses

1. Guy Winch, "#146—Guy Winch, PhD: Emotional First Aid and How to Treat
   Psychological Injuries," January 25, 2021, in *The Drive*, produced by Peter Attia,
   podcast, MP3 audio, 1:57:28, https://peterattiamd.com/guywinch/.
2. Dan P. McAdams, "'In the Beginning' and 'Once Upon a Time,'"
   TEDxHendrixCollege, Conway, Arkansas, April 29, 2012, YouTube video,
   15:37, https://www.youtube.com/watch?v=uxB3gSnMiNw.

Chapter 9: Food, Grief, and Other Distractions

1. "Ac-Cent-Tchu-Ate the Positive," featuring Jonny Mercer, written by
   Johnny Mercer and Harold Arlen, produced by Capitol Records, released
   October 4, 1944.
2. Liz Wright, "Gwendolyn Rogers's Bittersweet Path to the Cake Bake Shop,"
   Indianapolis Monthly, December 11, 2018, https://www.indianapolismonthly
   .com/longform/gwendolyn-rogers-bittersweet-path-to-the-cake-bake-shop.
3. *All Creatures Great and Small*, season 2, episode 7, "A Perfect Christmas,"
   written by Ben Vanstone, produced by Ben Vanstone, Melissa Gallant,
   and Colin Callender, aired December 24, 2021, on BBC, https://
   www.youtube.com/watch?v=ZbPCx3L6EIE.

Chapter 10: Small Favors, Thin Spaces

1. "We Are Climbing Jacob's Ladder," Hymnary.org, accessed May 12, 2022, https://hymnary.org/text/we_are_climbing_jacobs_ladder_we_are_cli.

Chapter 11: I'm Okay with Where I Am Today

1. "The Channel Tunnel," Eurostar, accessed June 20, 2023, https://www .eurostar.com/be-en/travel-info/eurostar-experience/the-channel-tunnel.
2. *Call the Midwife*, season 10, episode 5, written by Heidi Thomas, produced by Pippa Harris and Heidi Thomas, May 16, 2021, on BBC, https:// www.youtube.com/watch?v=oHoiOp3gYlo.
3. Dr. Paul Conti, *Trauma: The Invisible Epidemic* (Boulder, CO: Sounds True, 2021), 14.
4. Nedra Glover Tawwab (@nedratawwab), "It's okay to say, 'I'm not ready to share more at this time,'" Instagram, April 1, 2022, https://www.instagram .com/p/Cb0Ch91uOn6/.
5. Conti, *Trauma: The Invisible Epidemic*, 18.

Chapter 12: Continuing Education

1. Donald P. McNeill, Douglas A. Morrison, and Henri J. M. Nouwen, *Compassion: A Reflection on the Christian Life* (1982; repr., New York: Doubleday, 2006), 123.

Chapter 13: The Nightmare Ends

1. Rachel Yehuda and Amy Lehrner, "Intergenerational Transmission of Trauma Effects: Putative Role of Epigenetic Mechanisms," *World Psychiatry* 17, no. 3 (October 2018): 243–57, https://doi.org/10.1002%2Fwps.20568; Karina Margit Erdelyi, "Can Trauma Be Passed Down from One Generation to the Next?," Psycom, August 13, 2022, https://www.psycom.net/trauma /epigenetics-trauma.

ABOUT THE AUTHOR

CAROLE HOLIDAY SPENT TWENTY YEARS ON BUSINESS STAGES encouraging entrepreneurs. She subsequently owned a cooking school located in a turn-of-the-century cottage. At a season in life when many would retire, her daughter challenged her to write. She shares stories from years of shenanigans and serendipities and, yes, heartbreaks. Carole lives in Costa Mesa, California, happily surrounded by her grandchildren who still think she's really cool. She would respectfully ask you not to tell them otherwise.

COMPEL
Writers Training

COMPEL Writers Training is a faith-based online community from Lysa TerKeurst and Proverbs 31 Ministries. COMPEL was designed to help writers find direction for their work, receive practical training, and discover the motivation to keep going.

We've built COMPEL around three pillars:

- Community with other writers and COMPEL leaders.
- Content that is practical and inspiring.
- Connection with experts in the field and unique publishing opportunities.

SIGN UP TODAY AT COMPELTRAINING.COM

COMPEL
A WRITERS COMMUNITY FOUNDED BY
LYSA TERKEURST